Something
in This Book
Is True . . .

Something in This Book Is True . . .

The official companion to
NOTHING IN THIS BOOK IS TRUE, BUT IT'S EXACTLY HOW THINGS ARE

Bob Frissell

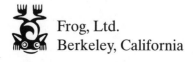
Frog, Ltd.
Berkeley, California

Frog, Ltd. books are distributed by
North Atlantic Books
P.O. Box 12327
Berkeley, California 94712

Cover art and illustrations pp. 8, 28, 44, 60, 196, 214 by Spain Rodriguez
Cover and book design by Paula Morrison
Typeset by Nancy Koerner

Printed in the United States of America.

Library of Congress Cataloging-in-Publication Data

Frissell, Bob, 1943–
    Something in this book is true / Bob Frissell.
       p. cm.
    ISBN: 1-883319-65-x
    1. Occultism. 2. Spiritual life. I. Title.
    BF1999.F745 1997
    033—dc21   97–15789
                                             CIP

2   3   4   5 / 01   00   99   98

Acknowledgments

Thank you Leonard Orr, and Drunvalo Melchizedek, for being the perfect catalysts, and for appearing at exactly the right time.

Thank you Alfred Lee, for all your computer help and for your watchful eye on the internet.

Thank you Kathy Glass, and Richard Grossinger, for your expert editing help. Thanks to everyone at North Atlantic Books, including Nancy Koerner, Paula Morrison, and Spain Rodriguez.

Thank you Brett Lilly, for your editing and legal help.

Thank you Joel Frissell, Werner Erhard, Brian Hall, Carol Kemp, Eileen Bray, Paul White, Carolyn, Ron and Carla Benson, Kim Edward Black, and Joyce Pinkerton.

Thank you Lois Cheesman, for typing, editing, researching, co-authoring, and doing whatever else it took to turn this book into a reality. And especially, thank you for your emotional support.

Contents

Introduction

One of the questions most frequently asked of me in the past two years has been, "When are you going to write another book?" For a long time, I had no answer. The book you are now holding has been some time in the making. I had to wait for the proper timing, for the motivation, the inspiration, for everything to come together. I didn't want to just crank out another book; I wanted to be sure I had something to say.

Because this is a time of tremendous change for all of us, both individually and collectively, the greatest need as I see it is first to give a clear understanding of just what is going on, and then to address how we can best align with and tune to this process of change.

Therefore, I use the first half of the book to paint the bigger picture, to fill in the blanks, to give background information, to update, and to continue where *Nothing* left off.

The theme I am expanding upon in *Something* is that when you step into the larger picture, when you begin to lift the veil so you can see more clearly, the process is obviously going to put you through some changes. One way I'm wording the issue is: "In the context of these changes—including the dimensional shift—it's not useful to be in fear; yet how do you deal with the fear that all these changes bring up for you?"

So the second half of the book is about emotional-body clearing, the process of learning to move consciously through your fears and limitations, which enables you more fully to step into the realization of who you are and why you're here —in the context of the bigger picture.

This book is based on the premise that you are part of and inseparable from the whole. It is about stepping into your personal power and discovering that you have everything you need, and it is all contained within.

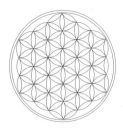

1

SOMETHING FROM NOTHING

One day in late October 1992, I received a phone call from a person who wanted to know about rebirthing. There was nothing particularly unusual about such a call. However, this person was very resistant and skeptical toward the process. That was unusual. A skeptical person usually doesn't call in the first place, or if they do, the conversation seldom lasts long.

We talked for about forty-five minutes. At one point this person, who had introduced himself as Richard, told me that he didn't believe in or trust the rebirthing process. He spoke of friends who had experienced something called rebirthing in 1968. Suffice it to say they had nothing good to say about it.

Why was this person calling, I wondered. I explained to him that rebirthing didn't even exist until 1974. I don't think he heard that.

To me, the most important aspect of the rebirthing process is what the person brings to it. One must be willing to do it in the first place, because out of such willingness comes a person's intention to go for the desired result. To me, such willingness and intention are what empower the entire process.

So I only play off a person's willingness. If it's there, great! If it isn't, I never try to force the issue because it never works.

I generally try to talk a skeptical person out of it—too much money, I'm too busy, or something. But for some reason, I just stayed with Richard, and for some reason, he decided to schedule an appointment.

He came on Wednesday, October 28, three days before Halloween, and one week before the election (the one in which Clinton defeated Bush). He brought his doubts with him.

He also brought a catalogue. He had told me on the phone that he was the publisher of North Atlantic Books, and he gave me a copy of the company catalogue. On the front cover was a one-square-inch picture of the "face on Mars."

The picture jumped out at me, but I said nothing. We were there to do a rebirthing session.

At some point, about halfway through the session, he had an experience of the process that was powerful enough to melt through his doubts and resistance. It was a shift as profound as any I had ever seen—a shift that, according to Richard, was only possible coming from a condition of doubt and no trust.

Now, for the first time, communication began to happen. After the session I could no longer contain my curiosity, so I asked about the face on Mars. Richard explained to me how North Atlantic came to be the publisher of Richard Hoagland's book, *The Monuments of Mars*.[1]

I immediately perked up, for we were now in the area of my greatest interest. It was only a few months earlier that I had discovered Drunvalo Melchizedek and his "Flower of Life" information. I had purchased a set of Drunvalo's videos, locked the door, taken the phone off the hook, and proceeded to learn the information to the best of my ability. Nothing else mattered.

So it was my natural inclination to share with Richard my knowledge of the face on Mars based on my understanding of Drunvalo's "Flower of Life" material. It was also my natural inclination to find out in as much detail as I could exactly what Richard knew.

Needless to say, a whole new possibility for our relationship was emerging. As we continued to talk, I learned that Richard was a great baseball fan and in fact had authored several books on the subject. This was very interesting to me, as I am also a great fan of baseball. In fact, I am convinced it is the one thing that kept me grounded throughout my many personal changes (stay tuned). No matter how crazy it got, there was always baseball to serve as some semblance of reality.

So, as it turns out, Richard grew up in New York as a devout fan of the Yankees until 1964. This was becoming *very* interesting, almost too good to be true. I too grew up a Yankee fan, at exactly the same time he did, though in North Dakota. I would have done anything to have seen the Yankees in my youth. Yogi, Mickey, Whitey, are you kidding? And here was Richard telling me he had done exactly that.

I even named one of my cats after Billy Martin. Billy, who was just about the mellowest cat you would ever want to meet, became my chief rebirthing assistant. He was present at every rebirthing session, including all of Richard's.

Richard returned the following Tuesday, November 3. It was election day. It was also Richard's birthday. In fact, he came for the next twenty-nine consecutive weeks. This was highly unusual. I see most clients for ten sessions and that's it.

We continued to talk about Mars. In fact, Richard even called me up on a few occasions just to talk about it. This is great, I thought. After all, who wouldn't want to talk about their favorite subject?

Then one day I came home to find a message on my answering machine. It was Richard. He wanted to know if I would be interested in writing a book on what he called the esoteric meaning of the Monuments on Mars. He went on to say that I may not feel like I was the right person to write the book, and that Richard Hoagland didn't either. "That's correct," I thought. In fact, I was convinced that I was the last person who should be considered for such an endeavor.

It should be pointed out that in our many discussions, I was not auditioning to write a book. In fact, I was avoiding it because of an experience I had in 1989. In July of that year a rebirthing client revealed to me that not only was she an author, but she was keeping a diary of her sessions. She showed it to me. What I saw was good—in fact, it was excellent! She was explaining, in a way I never could, just what it is like to go through a series of sessions. She then suggested that we co-author a book on the subject.

It sounded like a good idea to me in a way, and yet in a way it did not. Basically, what surfaced for me were my doubts: I was too busy, I didn't have anything unique to say. Simply stated, the timing wasn't right. Oh yes, I also knew it would be a lot of work.

Then I discovered that since we didn't have a publisher, we would first have to write a book proposal and then seek out and convince a publisher that we were worthy of being published. I knew I didn't want to do that, and I used it as a reason to say no. In fact, I decided then that I would not write a book until a publisher came to me and asked me.

So back to Richard's message, and it's good that it was a message. It gave me a chance to realize that even though my first response was "No, you must be kidding," something inside of me said, "Wait a minute, there are too many coincidences here, too many improbable alignments."

One thing I had learned for sure in my many years of rebirthing was to trust my inner guidance, my intuition.

I began to realize that the One Spirit had, for whatever reason, picked me to put this information out in book form. I did not try to make any of it happen, I didn't even want to do it, but I realized that it was something bigger than me, much bigger! I couldn't say no to that, and my first book, entitled *Nothing in This Book is True but It's Exactly How Things Are*, was born.

Sometime later, my nephew Joel wanted to know the title of my book. His mother told him. Now, Joel is autistic and one of his traits is repetition. You had better watch what you say in his presence because you are very likely to hear it again. Of course, upon hearing the title of my book he began repeating it. But then he did an internal about-face, as if the possibility that nothing in the book was true just couldn't be, and so he began repeating, "Something in this book is true!"

Upon hearing this, I instantly realized, "That's it! That is the title of my next book!" Thank you, Joel.

I am making progress—at least *something* in this book is true. So how do you write a book about something, especially if it is the "official" companion to *Nothing*? I see it as a continuation—it fills in the blanks, updates, and continues where *Nothing* left off.

Nothing was more about showing the mind the unity of being, whereas *Something* focuses on emotional-body clearing. This is pretty much the reverse of how I learned it.

My introduction to all of this came through what you might call emotional-body right-brain training, primarily through rebirthing. It began in 1979.

Twelve years later I was left with the question, "What's missing?" That's real progress. I had advanced to the point where I was aware in my conscious mind that something was missing. Prior to that time, I not only didn't know, but I didn't know that I didn't know!

This search for what was missing came to a head in January of 1991, and from there I was led on a journey of discovery that began to culminate in June of 1992 when I discovered Drunvalo Melchizedek and his Flower of Life information. Much of what Drunvalo presented was a modern-day version of an ancient Egyptian mystery school, the symbol for which was the Right Eye of Horus. The right eye is controlled by the left brain, so this was primarily male knowledge, the logical side of how everything in life is interconnected.

We all have what you might call a left-brain component of the mind and a right-brain component. This is true for both males and females. Our brains are further divided into four quadrants. The left side, or "left brain," has its logical component forward, and the right side, or "right brain," has its intuitive component forward, although the left side does have an intuitive aspect to it, the right side a logical aspect. These latter components form the two quadrants in the rear. The left brain is also known as the male side, while the right brain is known as the female side.

As Drunvalo has said, there's really no problem for us humans right now on the right side. Even though there is no "proof" to that effect, the right side is able to intuit that everything is interconnected. The problem, according to Drunvalo, is on the left side, because when it looks out into the world, all it sees is polarity and separation, polarity and separation all the way to the horizons of time and space. It needs to be shown, in the only way it can be shown, which is logically—that everything is totally and completely interlinked. Until then it will remain isolated; in fact, it has to be *convinced* beyond the slightest doubt. At that point, when it begins to merge with the right brain, a whole new possibility for awareness arises.

In Egypt, the prerequisite for the Right Eye of Horus mystery school was two-fold. One, (purely chronological) you had to be at least forty-five years of age, and two, you had to have twelve years of right-brain emotional-body training in a school known as the Left Eye of Horus.

Unknowingly and unwittingly, this is how I did it. I had no idea it was the Egyptian way until I met Drunvalo. It just turned out that way for me.

Again, I am presenting this information pretty much in reverse order. There is some advantage to this as I see it. Since we are so rooted in polarity consciousness, it might be necessary to first show the mind the illusory nature of duality and then work with the emotional body. I personally set the prerequisite that a person must have taken the Flower of Life workshop before I am willing to teach them rebirthing (*almost* always, since I am willing to make occasional exceptions based on my intuition). And I definitely set the requirement that they have at least read *Nothing*.

Okay. Now on to the big stuff. This book is based on the premise that you are part of and inseparable from the whole. There is One Spirit that moves through all life everywhere, including you. You gain access to it by going inside yourself. Instead of looking outside and giving your power away, you step into your personal power by discovering that you have everything you need, and it is all contained within.

I will tell you, mostly in story form, how it happened in my life, how I grew into the realization that there is a bigger picture, through a series of experiences—all of which utterly conflicted with my perception of reality. The outcome was that I knew for certain there is more going on than what appears on the surface. These experiences left me with the certainty that my life will never be the same!

It is my intent that this telling of my discovery will help create a pathway for you, so that your life may never be the same either.

Bon Voyage!

Notes

1. Richard C. Hoagland, *The Monuments of Mars: A City on the Edge of Forever* (Berkeley, CA: North Atlantic Books, 1987).

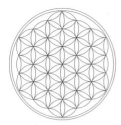

2

INITIATION

In 1979 I discovered Leonard Orr. One evening I went with two friends to his money seminar at his original rebirthing center, the Theta House in San Francisco. The seminar was held in the attic, the largest room in an old Victorian at 301 Lyon Street, across from the Panhandle, leading into Golden Gate Park.

Leonard was a big draw at the time, and the room was completely filled, probably seventy-five to eighty people. Each participant was given a multi-page essay called "The Prosperity Consciousness Consultation," written by Leonard. The seminar consisted of this essay being read aloud by various participants, followed by discussion of the ideas and questions it generated. Leonard, for the most part, just sat in the front of the room and smiled.

At one point we came to a negotiation section, and in it, Leonard gave everyone an opportunity to pay him extra, anywhere from one dollar to one hundred dollars. Considering that we had already paid fifteen dollars to attend the seminar, it seemed ridiculous to me that anyone in their right mind would want to pay anything more. It absolutely stunned me to sit there and watch people standing in line, waiting for the opportunity to pay Leonard more. And Leonard, who was wearing a green sweater with dollar signs all over it (no kidding) and sporting a freshly shaved head (I later discovered that this was a technique of spiritual purification passed straight to him by Babaji—more on that later), just sat there and smiled.

That was my introduction to Leonard. I decided I just had to go back and check it out again. This time, I went prepared to give Leonard an additional ten dollars. I don't know why— just to see what it felt like, I guess. So I went with twenty-five dollars, fifteen to get in the door plus an additional ten for "the Man." I came with a longtime friend, Ila. Just before we got to the negotiation section, I asked Ila if she had ten dollars I could borrow. I couldn't possibly give a logical explanation; I had just decided I wanted to go up and give Leonard *twenty* dollars instead of ten. Ila thought I was crazy, but she did pull out the ten dollars.

So, at the appropriate moment, I got in line with my twenty dollars. At the time, that was a lot of cash for me— thirty-five dollars when you count the fifteen to get in the door. I was not much of a wage hog. Long ago I had learned that my freedom was more important to me than money, especially if it meant doing something I didn't like. Spending the day in the redwoods or at the ocean was far more important than working.

I had learned that lesson well, but I was still what you might call "in transition." As Leonard would say, I was in the transition of working from conditioned motivation (a robot following instructions and reinforced by the money) to working from divine motivation (operating off your own authority where your work is not only your pleasure but an expression of your divine nature).

Again, Leonard was wearing his green $ sweater, his head freshly shaved. As I stood in line I felt doubts starting to creep in, like "This is crazy. What am I doing?" Then it was my turn to pay. I felt weird, embarrassed, stupid, intimidated, nervous, frightened, you name it! I could barely look at Leonard, yet I was somehow able to hand him the twenty dollars as he sat there and just smiled.

I later learned that Leonard was an absolute expert at that sort of thing. As he would explain it, whenever two or more people gather, there is always an exchange of energy. If the other person is more conscious than you are, what you will feel is your own energy, i.e., your own fears and limitations. When you get to the point where you can just "be" with that person, you have moved through or integrated that particular set of fears. That evening was my first introduction to what you might call "guru consciousness."

Later in the same evening Leonard announced that he would be conducting a year-long training program beginning in March 1980. The purpose of this program was to train rebirthers and seminar leaders, and for only one thousand dollars a month we would have the privilege of learning directly from him. I could barely give him twenty dollars— how could I ever give him one thousand? Of course, I ended up joining the program.

I also heard about Babaji for the first time and borrowed another ten dollars from Ila in order to purchase a poster of him, a poster that two years later would literally come to life!

I knew from that evening on that my life would never be the same. Yet as I would soon learn, Leonard has the ability to shatter your view of reality in a multitude of ways.

Of the many things I learned from Leonard, there is one area in particular that I wish I had never heard about. I spent many years wishing I had never had my eyes opened to this, even wishing I had never met Leonard, because he talked about something that was very disturbing, to say the least. This was the first indication I had that life is not what it appears to be, that there is something else going on, and it can scare you right out of your socks, especially if you only have partial information. What he was talking about were Earth changes.

Readers, put on your seat belts! But be aware, when I take you on a journey that's unsurvivable, I intend to be a responsible guide. No one's going to get obliterated on my watch. I will bring you all home in one piece, if you are willing. That's the key thing—you must be willing. Don't forget that for a moment as you read: the universe is big, but you are consciousness, which is bigger.

You see, I live in California, and that fact alone in this context is guaranteed to draw a laugh because you know what's going on aboard this terrestrial plate. Earthquakes are a fact of life. Not only earthquakes, but take your pick: In the dry months we have fires. In the wet months we have floods and mudslides—equally devastating. But Leonard was talking about something way beyond that. He was talking about an event which combines flood, earthquake, and cosmic fireworks as well. When you're naming stuff Earth changes rather than earthquakes you're summoning earthquakes that are off the scale. Ultimately we're talking about continents moving up and down—old ones disappearing and new ones surfacing. Enough already? No way! Beyond that even, we're talking about pole shifts! The planet unsheathing and resheathing electromagnetically. Not a gentle business at this wavelength.

Now, it would have been real easy—in fact, it would have been all too easy—to dismiss this as the product of someone's warped imagination. If you know Leonard that's pretty easy to do, but I trusted his ultimate sources. He was getting this information directly from two primary messengers: Not from reading a book, not from going to workshops, but via face-to-face contact. Leonard spent time with the Hopi Indians of the Third Mesa at Hotevilla, the ones who keep the old myths, and he learned from them directly just what Hopi prophecy means. I will briefly summarize it for readers who are not familiar with what's been coming out of Hoteville since the 1960s, *Saquasohuh* (Blue Star Kachina) and all. In essence, my interpretation of what they are saying resembles the old Chinese proverb: if we don't change our direction, we're liable to end up where we're headed. We have not been very conscious or careful caretakers of planet Earth. To the Hopi the planet is alive; it is a living body. Just as our bodies respond directly to how we treat them, as well as how we mistreat them, so does the planet. Consider for a moment how we mistreat our bodies. Just look at the most popular forms of death in our culture, heart disease and cancer. I could make a very solid argument that those are both a result of the accumulated mistreatment of the body. We know that if we continue to mistreat our body, it will start talking back in the form of earthquakes. We call them heart attacks. The planet is really similar. We've been abusing and misusing it for so long, thinking we're separate from it, trying to conquer it and control it. After a certain point, the planet starts talking back in the form of "heart attacks." We call them natural disasters. I think this is what the Hopi are talking about too; only they use the language of turkey and coyote spirits and dimensional realms separated by *sipápus* (the small hole in the floor, [of a kiva] represents the womb, the Place of Emergence from the preceding world).[1] Leonard visited the Hopi elders and got these prophecies firsthand. Of course, he would come back and tell us all about it.

The other primary source of Leonard's information was India. In the book *Autobiography of a Yogi*,[2] written by Paramahansa Yogananda, a chapter introduces "Babaji, the Yogi Christ of Modern India." Babaji was Leonard's other main source of Earth change information. Leonard used to go to India every year and spend at least one month at

Babaji's ashram, where he would receive the transmission directly.

Let me backtrack a little and tell you about Babaji. If you're familiar with Paramahansa Yogananda's book, and specifically that chapter, you know that we are talking about a pretty incredible person here, one who can manifest various bodies over a time period that greatly exceeds a normal lifespan. It's the sort of thing that we all think just can't happen, but Babaji demonstrates for us that it does. So obviously this is not your normal everyday person.

My understanding of Babaji is that he always has the ability to have a body, in fact, to manifest one instantly. He doesn't have to go through the birth process like us. When he wants a body he snaps his finger and there's a body. He can step into a new body any time he wants. It has also been my understanding that he usually does not make himself available to the public. In fact, I've heard stories of how he would be living in a village where many if not most of the villagers didn't know who he was. But for the time period from 1970 to 1984, he did make himself more available. One day he just appeared out of a cave. He had manifested the body of an eighteen-year-old in the cave and just walked out and set up his ashram for a period of fourteen years. One of the people to find out about this appearance was Leonard; eventually many of the early rebirthers went on a yearly pilgrimage to India and heard fascinating and incredible stories. These included Earth change prophecies.

Babaji was talking about ninety percent of the Earth's population being removed via Earth changes, entire continents going up and down. For those of you who wonder about a continent called Atlantis, traditional wisdom holds it that it sank in this manner (from continental shift) with about sixty-four million citizens. This great loss of life is recorded in an ancient Mayan document, the *Troano Manuscript:*

In the year 6 Kan, on the 11 Muluc, in the month of Zac,
there occurred terrific earthquakes which continued until
the 13 Chuen without interruption. *The country of the
hills of earth—the land . . .* was sacrificed. Being *twice*
upheaved, it disappeared during the night, being constantly shaken by the fires of the underneath. Being con-
fined, these caused the land to rise and to sink several
times in *various places*. At the last the surface gave way
and the ten countries (or tribes) were torn asunder and
scattered. They sank with their 64,000,000 inhabitants.[3]

For me, all this was really the first indicator that life is not
as it appears to be out there, that there is something else
going on. But I had only partial information. My aim is not
to leave you with partial information, because if that's all
you have it can be terminally frightening.

The sources of these historical legends and Earth prophecies are venerable. The Hopi have been around a long time
and Babaji's no latecomer either. So when they speak, I listen. They're all saying the same thing, that it's going to happen right about now, in the late 1990s.

In December of 1981, Leonard came to the Theta House in
San Francisco. The Theta House was at that time the local
rebirthing center. I was a staff member there, but whether I
was or not I still would have gone to hear Leonard speak.
He arrived a couple of weeks before Christmas to give a new
seminar on what he called the spiritual interpretation of Han-
del's *Messiah*. I thought that sounded interesting and I wanted
to see Leonard anyway. In addition to his scheduled topic,
he handed out a five- or six-page essay.

This essay was entitled "Rebirth of the Late Great Planet
Earth." He went into great detail about Earth changes that
were going to happen in California, and he said they were

going to happen in the year 1982. Again, I could have thought, "Well, that's just Leonard," but I didn't. I took it seriously and began to wonder: What would life be like if all of a sudden you couldn't go to the supermarket anymore? What good is your car going to do you if you can't fill it with fuel? What good is a bank account if the banks are closed? Leonard was talking about all these things and more, and he said they were going to occur in 1982.

Well, it just so happened that in the first four or five days of January in 1982, there were torrential rain storms in the San Francisco Bay Area. It rained so much and the mudslides were so intense that their combined effect closed the road going to the canyon near where I lived, and that road has been closed ever since. Entire hills were displaced.

I also vividly remember a pool of mud on one of the trails in this area, a virtual lake of mud. For some reason, a person on horseback tried to ride his horse right through the middle of that mud and started sinking as if it were quicksand. It's just one of those things that is so incredible you can't believe it is happening. That horse kept sinking all the way up to its neck. I don't know how they got him out. That the sort of thing leaves an impression on you. So I started thinking maybe Leonard is really onto something here; I began taking this information even more seriously.

I recall hiking with friends and wondering out loud what life would be like without supermarkets. Can we eat these berries, or are they poisonous? How about these leaves? Obviously the deer and the wild animals know how to make it. Maybe it would be a good idea for us to learn too.

I started collecting any available information on Earth changes. There was one author named Moira Timms who was giving chapter and verse on these sorts of things. After a few months, I felt like an ostrich taking his head out of the sand, wondering if it's okay to stay up, hoping that maybe it's not really going to happen this year. I guess I was too deeply into it at first to notice, but after a few months I became aware that I was in the middle of a very profound, powerful process whereby my "stuff," namely my unconscious fears, was coming to the surface in droves. If you are at all like me, what you normally do is try to keep these fears and limitations buried as deeply as possible. Leonard's essay and my subsequent research worked like dynamite charges.

As I began to notice my personal process, I realized that as I confronted my fears and limitations they began to integrate. Not only did I integrate this new knowledge without freaking out, I became empowered by it. As I came to terms with previously unconscious fears, I experienced profound personal changes. To put it simply, I was coming more fully into my own personal power. At the time, I was self-employed as a rebirther and workshop leader. It's extremely useful if you're self-employed, especially doing this type of work, leading others, to integrate and move through your own fears and limitations. This was what I call "phase one" of my process of transforming my fears relating to the survival of the planet.

But the bar was soon raised. I got another jolt in 1986 from an ascended master named Ramtha who channels through a woman by the name of JZ Knight. In an eight-hour video of JZ Knight channeling Ramtha, entitled "Changes,"4 guess what the focus was? Ramtha was mapping the exact same scenario as Leonard, saying dramatic Earth changes were going to happen in the 1986 or 1987 time frame. I went through my whole fear process all over again. When this one finally integrated, I began to notice I had moved through a whole new layer of fears and limitations that had been even more deeply buried, and that I had become even more grounded and connected with my personal power. This is an interesting process. The more fears assault consciousness, the more awesome the fears, the more potential for growth. This is the only way. It has probably always been the only way. The universe needs to wake us up in order to change us.

So, after allowing myself to confront and assimilate this information for a long time, the main thing I noticed was my own personal process evolving. Far from this scary stuff being a bane to my existence, it had enormous, almost incalculable value.

Jumping ahead to January 1991, I now had twelve years exactly, give or take a week, of sometimes unwilling emotional-body training, specifically through the process called rebirthing—with great assistance, I might add, from Leonard, Ramtha, and all the Earth change prophecies. But while I had twelve real years of legitimate emotional-body clearing, I didn't think anything of it. Twelve years didn't really mean anything to me and I had no idea, absolutely no idea, that the mystery schools did almost this exact same thing for twelve years back in ancient Egypt. I didn't have perspective yet. But what I did notice after twelve years of one kind of emotional-body clearing was that something was missing. I noticed a lack more than anything else.

It is important for me to make this point here because you would think that after moving through major fears and limitations and clearing yourself out emotionally—which involves the right-brain side, the intuitive side—you would be on cloud nine and feeling very spiritual and loving towards everyone. I didn't. I felt an emptiness. And this gap was stronger than anything I had ever felt in my life. It got to the point where I felt it in every cell of my body and I desperately wanted to know what the missing piece was.

There is a principle involved here. Very simply, if you want to know something badly enough, you will be shown the way.

The universe is always one hundred percent on purpose. It's creating itself over and over again in perfect harmony. I even get the impression that it "knows" what it is doing. The problem is, for the most part we don't conduct our wills in a purposeful way, so we don't notice the deep personal alignment that we have with the universe, and we end up thinking the universe doesn't support us. Yet the universe supports us unerringly. If we're off purpose, then it's supporting us unerringly in being off purpose. Instant feedback! It's putting a mirror up there for us, and what we see always is ourselves. So if we are off purpose that is what is reflected back.

Well, for the first time in my life I was "on purpose" in every cell of my body. The universe in its infinite wisdom noticed that and began to give me exactly what I was asking for. I didn't have to go anywhere. I didn't have to do anything. The missing piece magically began to appear before me.

In January of 1991, I was at Leonard Orr's present rebirthing center, Campbell Hot Springs, leading a week-long training. While at the center, I had seen a particular person, Doug, at various times throughout the course of the week— meeting him on the trail, passing him to and from the lodge. I would say hi but we never got beyond that. I didn't even know his name until later in the week. Then on Friday, before going to do the evening seminar, I happened to stop in the lunchroom. The room was empty and there was nobody to talk to, so I got a snack and looked for something to read.

Well, I found something all right, and the second I laid eyes on it, I realized the "here we go again, my life will never be the same" scenario was about to repeat itself. The book I had picked up was about extra-terrestrial involvement on our planet, something I had never really thought about before. I had always put it out of my mind, or regarded it as fantasy, science fiction, or tabloid invention. But here this book was, spelling it out in black and white, in particular introducing a

race called the Greys, little three-and-a-half to four-foot-tall
guys with the big bug eyes who are abducting us, mutilating
cattle, and carrying out all manner of amoral mischief. The
book went into great detail about this. It also went into detail
about our government's knowledge of and intimate involvement with the Greys, including their secret involvement, *and
even our secret government's secret involvement.*

I have been interested in politics ever since I was maybe
eleven or twelve years old. I can remember in 1956, sitting
down and watching each political convention, Republicans
and Democrats, practically from gavel to gavel. Not every
twelve-year-old thinks this is the most fascinating thing there
is. But I had this tremendous attraction to it. Later, for example, I knew on some level that the Watergate cover-up was
successful, and I suppose just to prove to people how smart
I was, my pet phrase of the time became "the cover-up
worked." I didn't *really* know what I was saying back in 1973.
But by January of 1992, I began to get an idea of what my
own phrase "the cover-up worked" meant and it totally,
absolutely blew my mind. Once more I realized, here we go
again, my life will never ever be the same.

It would have been all too easy to dismiss this information as the product of some kook, somebody who is writing
a book just for the purpose of making money. Of course,
books like that don't seem to sell too well, right? But I did
not dismiss the information. One of the many things I had
learned in twelve years of emotional-body clearing was to
trust my intuition, the part of the brain—the right side— that
can't prove something but is able to "feel" and is able to
"tune." I trusted my intuition. This information was con-
veying details about people that we all know, very famous
people, such as presidents, cabinet members, and senators.
If I were to mention some of the names, you would definitely
recognize them.

Although my intuitive side said "yes, there is something to this," it was also the sort of thing that got me activated again. In case you haven't figured this out by now, "being activated" means all your fears and whatever you have been avoiding and resisting come to the surface: all of a sudden you can't keep "it" down anymore, it's like you are swimming in it. So here we go again. I had to lead the workshop that night, but I couldn't wait until it was over because I knew it was this guy Doug who had put this information out on the table in the lunchroom. I just had to meet him.

As soon as the workshop was over, I went out the door and there, courtesy of the universe, was Doug! I cornered him and we talked for hours. In January at 6000 feet in California, it does get cold. The seminar room may have been warm but the space where we were talking was cold—it was freezing cold—but it didn't matter. We sat in the cold for at least two or three hours and I pumped him with detailed questions, rapid fire, one after another.

The great thing was that he wanted to talk to me just as much as I wanted to talk to him—it was perfect. Finally it was time to call it a night and go to bed. Just as I was turning, he said, "Oh by the way, here's some more information for you." So I went up to my room and sat up all night reading. I might have gotten an hour's sleep, probably not, but I couldn't put that stuff down. Doug also said he had a bunch of videos and we could spend the next day watching them. That's exactly what we did, one after another, until I was so loaded with this information, I couldn't think about anything else.

So again, the information from Doug was still partial information, and it certainly can scare you if you take it as seriously as I did. To give you an indication how activated I was at the time, I remember driving home from Campbell Hot Springs. This was January of 1991, and on January 15,

1991, we physically attacked Iraq and the Gulf War began. That sent me off the chart.

I already felt that it was too late in terms of us taking care of the planet. What I mean is that I suspected we had used the planet up to the point where it was only a matter of time before the biosphere would no longer be able to support life. Now that's a pretty heavy-duty statement. How many of us have really thought that we could use this planet up to the point where it would no longer support life of any kind? Let me just throw out a couple of bits of information. Sometime around the turn of the century, there were roughly thirty million different species on the planet. But there are less than half that many right now, somewhere in the neighborhood of fourteen to fifteen million different species. If you could observe what's happening on this planet from a higher dimension, you would see that this level of the planet is rapidly dying. Now I don't want to leave you freaked out, because there is something else going on. There is a bigger picture here so you don't have to get stuck in fear, but I do recommend that you be concerned on some level, because everything is a function of consciousness and it really is up to us. It's in our best interest to wake up and become more conscious caretakers of our environment and to live in harmony with the Earth, because trying to conquer and control it doesn't work at any dimensional level.

I really thought that it was too late, but I was holding onto the last ray of hope—that by some miracle, we could all of a sudden see the error of our ways, understand what the Hopi have been telling us, and begin in unison (which is what it would have taken) to say we're not going to do this anymore. We're going to start living in harmony with the planet rather than in opposition to it. What did we do instead? On January 15 we attacked Iraq; then the oil fields were set on fire. It was an ecological and human disaster.

They still haven't told us ten percent of what happened over there.

My drive home from Campbell Hot Springs was a distance of about 240 miles and it took about four hours. Right in the middle of all of this, traveling down the freeway, I felt as though just about everybody on that freeway was in some way showing their support for the war. I was among lemmings. Now, I want to say this carefully. I thought that was the last straw that would break the camel's back. Yeah, we acted in unison, but in support of disaster, not in support of healing the planet. That's the way I saw it. I never felt more isolated—I was ashamed and embarrassed to be a member of the human race. I experienced a polarity gap wider than at any other moment. There was just no place to hide. It seemed as though everybody was in total support of disaster. I was ready to leave the planet, to go to Saturn or Mars or someplace, preferably in another solar system, or through the *sipápu*.

From then for a period of fifteen to eighteen months I felt my polarity gap growing wider and wider. Again, I had just finished twelve years of emotional-body training. You're supposed to feel exhilarated and loving to everyone and everything, yet I never felt more alienated in my life. The reason for that seeming contradiction is clear to me now. There was missing information. Until you get it all, you're dealing with incomplete information, and if it is dark-side information, as much of this was, it can really do a number on you.

This all came to a head in April of 1992. One day a new rebirthing client came to me. We sat and talked for a while, and he noticed a book on my table about crop circles. So we started discussing that subject. Then, out of the blue, he asked me if I had heard of Gordon-Michael Scallion. I said no, I hadn't heard of him, and who was he? He told me Gordon-Michael Scallion is a futurist talking about Earth changes with an eighty-seven percent accuracy rating. He then went on to tell me that Scallion had successfully predicted the Loma Prieta earthquake, the one we had in the San Francisco Bay Area in 1989.

We talked about Scallion and his predictions for about half an hour or so, until I got to the point where every submerged fear in my body came to the surface. I didn't even know I had that much left. And now I had to rebirth my client. Are you kidding me? It definitely should have been him rebirthing me! I faked my way through that one. Then, of course, glutton for punishment that I am, I had to go out and learn more about Gordon-Michael Scallion. I subscribed to his monthly newsletter called *The Earth Changes Report*. If you want this in your mailbox you'd better be prepared for a shock every month, because he is talking heavy-duty stuff.

At that time, Scallion was predicting the eventual fracture of California. Since this is literally the disintegration of the state I live in, I took it personally. Scallion's prediction was that the breaking apart of California would progress in three stages, the first to begin in June of 1992. Scallion said there were going to be two earthquakes in southern California. One was a 7.4—just as he predicted. It was later called the Landers Quake. He predicted another quake shortly thereafter, and a week or so later the Earth shook instruments at 6.5, just as he said.

Scallion claimed that these represented the initial stages in the fracturing of California. The San Francisco *Chronicle*[5] even reported something of the kind. I was real serious about it at that point. This would eventually lead to what Scallion called the Isles of California. He came out with a new map of the United States that shows Denver as a West Coast seaport. On that map, California is nothing but a series of islands.

I've lived in the Bay Area since 1971, and for the first twenty-two or twenty-three years, I lived either near or on the Hayward Fault, which runs up and down the East Bay. An earthquake on that fault line to the tune of 7.0 or greater would be devastating because there are at least a million and a half people who live along this fault. All the years I lived there I never thought a thing of it. If you reside here you just kind of live with it. That's just the way it is. Nobody really thinks it's going to happen, or if it does, you're going to be okay, or it will be centuries in the future, given geologic time and all. For the first time, I did not feel safe living in California. For the first time, I was also considering leaving. But I know that if you're motivated by fear, and if you're leaving for fear of earthquakes or other Earth changes, you're probably going to have a car accident on the way out of town. You can't run from fear; it doesn't work.

That's how things came to a complete head for me, as a result of partial information. I knew too much at that point, yet I didn't know enough. I didn't have the larger picture.

Another point really has to be made regarding Earth change prophecies. The purpose of any prophet, any person putting clear information out—be it the Hopi elders, Babaji, Edgar Cayce, Nostradamus, or Gordon-Michael Scallion—is to be wrong. Certainly if they are right, they can't go blowing their horn too much about it! So what I mean when I say their purpose is to be wrong is that they serve the universe by alerting us to the consequences of our mindless actions.

Any prophet's purpose is to deliver a wake-up call so that we can see what we've been doing. If we heed the prophecy, we can turn around—make an about-face—and by consciously seeing where we're headed we can see that we don't have to go there. Because everything is a function of consciousness, we can begin to move in a way that is more aware and more in harmony with life. In so doing, we can avoid the predicted outcome of these prophecies. We can become conscious enough and live harmoniously enough to prevent them. To me that is the purpose of a prophet. And if you take warnings as seriously as I did, you'll begin to notice that you go through an intensely powerful process. You also begin to notice that it is enormously to your advantage not to flee but to move through your fears and limitations. This is what emotional-body training is. You are broken open. Then you deepen. Then you become who you are.

We are now up to June of 1992, a time at which I was totally plugged into my fears. Colorado was my likely destination. (That's all they needed in Colorado, another Californian fleeing to the Rockies.) Instead, I decided to at least get off the Hayward Fault. I now live on the San Andreas Fault!

More importantly, I began to tune into and receive the missing information. By June of 1992 I desperately needed some relief, and it came. It arrived by the same old universal principle: If you want something badly enough, you don't have to go anywhere or do anything. All I had to do was go to my mailbox. There I found a letter, which I printed in my last book, on page six. It's the sort of communication that if you went around displaying it to most people, they would no longer *think* you're a kook, they would have proof positive. "That's it," they'd say. "This dude is reading mail like that and taking it seriously, he needs to be locked away."

But before I explain where this seemingly kooky letter led me in June of 1992, it is important for you to understand in more detail what I knew about prophecies and Earth changes.

Notes

1. Frank Waters, *Book of the Hopi* (New York: Penguin Books, 1963), p. 24.

2. Paramahansa Yogananda, *Autobiography of a Yogi* (Los Angeles, CA: Self-Realization Fellowship, 1946).

3. Col. James Churchward, *The Lost Continent of Mu* (New York: William Edwin Rudge, 1926; Essex, England: C. W. Daniel Co. Ltd., & Albuquerque, NM: BE Books, 1994), p. 52.

4. JZ Knight, "Changes" (Yelm, WA: Ramtha Dialogues, 1986), video.

5. Charles Petit, *Chronicle* Science Writer, "Fault Caught in Act of Forming," San Francisco *Chronicle*, July 3, 1992.

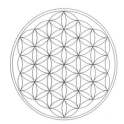

3

PROPHECIES

The Grand Alignment

In his essay "The Rebirth of the Late Great Planet Earth," Leonard wrote that in 1982 all the planets of the solar system would line up simultaneously on the same side of the sun.

He also mentioned this event in his book *Physical Immortality—The Science of Everlasting Life:*

> It is the opinion of some scientists that this lineup will cause huge tidal waves as high as 1,000 feet all over the earth which would virtually wipe out human life on all coastal cities. Some scientists have expressed the opinion that old continents may rise out of the ocean, which would sink huge portions of existing continents under water, e.g., it is predicted that the western half of the United States will be covered with water. Such major changes in the shape of the earth obviously could bring about massive earthquakes and all kinds of natural disasters. Some scientists believe that this lineup of all the planets on one side of the sun may temporarily bring about dramatic weather changes all over the earth. It is also just as possible that nothing dramatic will happen.[1]

Moira Timms also spoke of this 1982 configuration in *Prophecies and Predictions:*

> The external astronomical influence most likely to affect the stability of terra firma in the near future is a configuration which occurs once every 179 years. Around 1982 the nine planets of the solar system will be observed on the same side of the sun. They will not be in *exact* alignment at that time, but close enough to create intense influence. The combined gravitational pull will actuate strong tides and induce great magnetic storm flares on the sun, which will already be at the peak of its 11-year cycle. Again, we stress that sunspot cycles are motivators in human consciousness and affairs, having profound and little-understood psychological influence upon the group mind. Increased solar behavior during that time will surely affect global weather and could act to reduce the high-altitude West-to-East winds, the circumpolar vortex. If this happens it will drastically change the direction of the Earth's surface winds, further decelerate its rotation and precipitate earthquakes. This vortex has already undergone changes which have brought disastrous weather changes to many parts of the world. It doubled speed after the last and largest-ever burst of solar storms which arrived, out of phase and unexpectedly, in 1972 and 1978. Solar anomalies are likely to increase in intensity in the coming years.
>
> The recent publication, *The Jupiter Effect* (Walker & Co., NY) by astronomers Gribbin and Plagemann, confirmed information already known to metaphysicians for decades. They state that the aforementioned stresses will produce severe geostrophic strain on the world's weak or unstable areas. Changes in the position of the geographic poles have been recorded at least four times

during this century after major earthquakes. The scientists tell us that the 1982 alignment phenomenon will cause the planet to wobble on its axis, slowing the rotation and generating a jolt likely to trigger massive earthquakes and even a change in pole position.

There is special concern for California, situated on the San Andreas and other fault systems and already overdue for seismic relief. Each of the eight large earthquakes in the San Francisco area since 1836 has occurred within the two years following a period of intense sunspotting. It is the present increasing combination of anomalies, internal and external to the Earth, which conspire to make this particular occurrence of the nine-planet configuration so potentially cataclysmic.[2]

Timms went on to say that Nostradamus, Edgar Cayce, and Paramahansa Yogananda all had predicted great earthquakes before the end of the century, and that Jeanne Dixon also spoke of a major catastrophe for 1983.[3]

This book by Moira Timms became my personal companion and activator for the early months of 1982. It gave credence to much of what Leonard was saying. It also served as my introduction to many new ideas; *yugas,* the precession of the equinoxes, and the ultimate disaster—pole shifts! There was also a chapter on an old favorite, prophecies of the Hopi Indians.

The Hopi

A proud and peaceful nation, who probably have one of the most advanced cultures on the planet, the Hopi have lived 8in peace and harmony with Mother Earth for more than 10,000 years. They do not see themselves as separate from the Earth, but one with it. As I noted earlier, they see the Earth as a living organism—the trees, rocks, water, and the Hopi people are all one.

Timms told of how the Great Spirit entrusted to the Hopi an area of land known as Black Mesa for safekeeping and for posterity. According to the Great Spirit, this land was the spiritual center of the continent. It was meant to be a holy place, to be tended with great care and reverence in order that the balance of nature be preserved for the entire planet.

Even though this land (now known as the Four Corners because surveyors ran four American states together there) is arid and contains mostly rock and sand with few trees, the Hopi have for generations grown crops of corn, beans, and squash while grazing sheep and goats.

The Four Corners area is one of the few key focal centers in the world where the energy currents must be kept in balance to maintain the biosphere. Scientists are discovering that this area is unique with its combination of radioactive minerals, underground streams, and solar radiation. It is one of the main sources of positive and negative ions in the atmosphere, which are essential to the health and well-being of all life.[4]

The following Hopi prophecy was first published in a mimeographed manuscript that circulated among several Methodist and Presbyterian churches in 1959. The account begins by describing how while driving along a desert highway one hot day in the summer of 1958, a minister named David Young stopped to offer a ride to an Indian elder, who accepted with a nod. After riding in silence for several minutes, the Indian said:

> . . . "I am White Feather, a Hopi of the ancient Bear Clan. In my long life I have traveled through this land, seeking out my brothers, and learning from them many things full of wisdom. I have followed the sacred paths of my people, who inhabit the forests and many lakes

in the east, the land of ice and long nights in the north, and the places of holy altars of stone built many years ago by my brothers' fathers in the south. From all these I have heard the stories of the past, and the prophecies of the future. Today, many of the prophecies have turned to stories, and few are left—the past grows longer, and the future grows shorter.

And now White Feather is dying. His sons have all joined his ancestors, and soon he too shall be with them. But there is no one left, no one to recite and pass on the ancient wisdom. My people have tired of the old ways—the great ceremonies that tell of our origins, of our emergence into the Fourth World, are almost all abandoned, forgotten, yet even this has been foretold. The time grows short.

My people await Pahana, the lost White Brother [from the stars], as do all our brothers in the land. He will not be like the white men we know now, who are cruel and greedy. We were told of their coming long ago. But still we await Pahana.

He will bring with him the symbols, and the missing piece of that sacred tablet now kept by the elders, given to him when he left, that shall identify him as our True White Brother.

The Fourth World shall end soon, and the Fifth World will begin. This the elders everywhere know. The Signs over many years have been fulfilled, and so few are left.

This is the First Sign: We are told of the coming of the white-skinned men, like Pahana, but not living like Pahana—men who took the land that was not theirs. And men who struck their enemies with thunder.

This is the Second Sign: Our lands will see the coming of spinning wheels filled with voices. In his youth, my father saw this prophecy come true with his eyes—

the white men bringing their families in wagons across the prairies.

This is the Third Sign: A strange beast like a buffalo but with great long horns will overrun the land in large numbers. These White Feather saw with his eyes—the coming of the white men's cattle.

This is the Fourth Sign: The land will be crossed by snakes of iron.

This is the Fifth Sign: The land shall be criss-crossed by a giant spider's web.

This is the Sixth Sign: The land shall be criss-crossed with rivers of stone that make pictures in the sun.

This is the Seventh Sign: You will hear of the sea turning black, and many living things dying because of it.

This is the Eighth Sign: You will see many youth, who wear their hair long like my people, come and join the tribal nations, to learn their ways and wisdom.

And this is the Ninth and Last Sign: You will hear of a dwelling-place in the heavens, above the earth, that shall fall with a great crash. It will appear as a blue star. Very soon after this, the ceremonies of my people will cease.

These are the Signs that great destruction is coming. The world shall rock to and fro. The white man will battle against other people in other lands—with those who possessed the first light of wisdom. There will be many columns of smoke and fire such as White Feather has seen the white man make in the deserts not far from here. Only those which come will cause disease and a great dying. Many of my people, understanding the prophecies, shall be safe. Those who stay and live in the places of my people also shall be safe. Then there will be much to rebuild. And soon—very soon afterward—

Pahana will return. He shall bring with him the dawn
of the Fifth World. He shall plant the seeds of his wisdom in their hearts. Even now the seeds are being
planted. These shall smooth the way to the Emergence
into the Fifth World.

But White Feather shall not see it. I am old and dying.
You—perhaps will see it. In time, in time. . . ."

The old Indian fell silent. They had arrived at his destination, and Reverend David Young stopped to let him
out of the car. They never met again. Reverend Young
died in 1976, so he did not live to see the further ful-
fillment of this remarkable prophecy.

The signs are interpreted as follows: The First Sign is
of guns. The Second Sign is of the pioneer's covered
wagons. The Third Sign is of longhorn cattle. The Fourth
Sign describes the railroad tracks. The Fifth Sign is a
clear image of our electric power and telephone lines.
The Sixth Sign describes concrete highways and their
mirage-producing effects. The Seventh Sign foretells of
oil spills in the ocean. The Eighth Sign clearly indicates
the "Hippie Movement" of the 1960s. The Ninth Sign
was the U.S. Space Station Skylab, which fell to Earth
in 1979. According to Australian eye-witnesses, it
appeared to be burning blue.[5]

Ramtha

I first heard of Ramtha in 1985 from friends in the rebirthing
community. I had seen portions of his videos and was interested enough to explore further. A metaphysical bookstore
in Marin County was renting Ramtha videos so I decided to
go and check one of them out. Paper Ships, located in San
Anselmo, was a fantastic place, so small you barely had room

to turn around, yet filled with "goodies" that no one else had, including Ramtha videos for rent. The owner, David, with whom I was to reconnect eight years later when I discovered my first book was their best seller, suggested one particular video, called "Changes."[6] As usual I had no idea what I was getting into.

What I recall most clearly from the video was the presence of Ramtha himself, coming from unconditional love, and with great certainty, explaining in detail how we were due for major changes ... and soon.

He cited the wisdom of the ant, how they act in unison, storing food in preparation for the winter. He suggested we do likewise.

Ramtha indicated that this period of upheaval would be two years. He told in detail of the unsafe areas (mainly western United States), and he spoke of the wisdom of not being on the "zipper" when it opens. Great, I thought, California is nothing but zippers!

Gordon-Michael Scallion

The first issue of Gordon-Michael Scallion's monthly publication, *The Earth Changes Report*, came out in October 1991. In that venue, Scallion reported that since a key early warning sign had already occurred—namely two quakes in the Eureka, California, area in the six-magnitude range—he expected the area from Eureka to Bakersfield to become very active. He said this would be a prelude to several big ones in 1992.

In the January 1992 issue, an article written by Diana Leafe Christian gave more specific information. The article stated that beginning in August 1991, there would be twenty months at most before really large California quakes began, and that Los Angeles would be first. There were to be three earthquakes in the Los Angeles area, the third being the largest—an 8+ on the Richter scale.

Scallion then saw giant earthquakes occurring in the San Diego and San Francisco areas within three to thirty months of the first Los Angeles quake. He said the San Francisco area was in a cycle of three earthquakes, the first being the Loma Prieta 7.0 quake of October 17, 1989. The second quake was to be in the high 8's or low 9's, and the third Bay Area quake was to be in the 10 or 11 range.

He also saw what Edgar Cayce called "the breaking up of California" occurring sometime after the final San Francisco Bay Area quake. To quote directly from the article:

> Gordon-Michael calls this event a "fracture" because that is literally what will happen. In an earthquake that will be "off the chart"—a 15 on the Richter scale—a line from Eureka to Bakersfield, and pivoting southwest from Bakersfield to Baja California, will crack open, creating a giant fissure in the earth running the length of the San Joaquin and Sacramento Valleys. The land to the west of the fracture—a long segment of California from the fracture line to the seacoast—will then move independently of the rest of North America. It will rotate longitudinally along its north-south axis, and tilt upwards along the fracture line. The broken-off segment's western, seacoast edge will thus drop in elevation. As it drops, the Pacific ocean will move inland, covering more and more of the land up to approximately the fracture line. This whole segment will thus slide into the sea.
>
> An earthquake of such magnitude will cause several things simultaneously:
> • Tidal waves (tsunamis) going out across the Pacific.
> • A sonic or shock wave going east across North America.

• The shock wave will vibrate or oscillate the sediment layers beneath the Sierra Nevada and Rocky Mountain ranges, causing them to drop in altitude, with much damage there.

• The fissure or fracture line will become California's new seacoast.[7]

According to Scallion, certain portions of California would remain as islands and be known as "the Isles of California." He also said that this would be the first of three new western seacoasts of North America; that after two more fractures the final seacoast would follow a line from southwest Nebraska to northwest Arizona. Phoenix would become a seaport.

Scallion said that a huge magma bubble is pushing up beneath the United States and is the cause of the three-stage break-up of California. He said the magma bubble is being created by a massive build-up of ice at the poles which is causing the Earth's rotation to become unstable, which, in turn, is creating instability in the Earth's magma and core.

On April 22, 1992, a 6+-magnitude earthquake hit an area 110 miles east-southeast of Los Angeles. Scallion had earlier targeted April 17–22 as a 50% potential time frame for a quake in that area. He considered this to be the first of the three Los Angeles area quakes.

The May 1992 issue called for multiple earthquakes in the 6- to 8-magnitude range to hit California between May 8 and July 13, 1992. Scallion then gave an update on the California "fracture" from the period of May 8, 1992, to May 8, 1993:

First of a series of California fractures occur—9–19+ on the Richter Scale. Sections of land along the "fracture" line from Eureka to Bakersfield to the Baja separate. Gaps occur along this line from several feet to hundreds of feet. Fire leaps into the atmosphere as gases caused by electromagnetic forces ignite from fallen electric lines. The flames, blue-red in color, will be seen for hundreds of miles as they reach heights of 100 feet and more. Much of the coastal area of California floods and some islands are formed as a result. Property damage in San Diego, Los Angeles, and San Francisco will be in the trillions of dollars. The insurance industry collapses, U.S. economy fails, depression in U.S. Mass migrations to Nevada, Arizona, Colorado, and New Mexico.[8]

Scallion then said that if the May 8–July 13, 1992, scenario occurred, he would give a 65% probability of the first fracture to occur between June 17 to July 13, 1992. He added a 95% probability that the first fracture would occur no later than May 8, 1993.

Again, this was to be only the first of three fractures, the final tear occurring by September–December 1995, after which California becomes islands. He said he would be better able to fix this date after July 13, 1992.

In June 1992, Scallion gave a 65% probability of the second of the three Los Angeles quakes occurring in June or July of that year. He said the epicenter would be 120 to 150 miles southeast of Los Angeles with a magnitude in the range of 7.6, plus or minus 0.4. He also predicted a 7.8–8.2 quake in the Sonoma area of Northern California within 120 days.

On June 28, 1992, a 7.5 earthquake hit Landers, California. This quake, located 130 miles east of Los Angeles, ruptured the land for 44 miles. This rupture was reported in the San Francisco *Chronicle*.[9] Scallion said:

This is a very significant event, as the June 28th rupture zone parallels the "California Fracture" line prediction. In my prophecies I state that California will, in the '92–'97 time period, experience "super-mega-quakes"—magnitudes 10–15—breaking California into islands. . . . However, before this happens, according to the prophecies, three quakes will occur in L.A. The first was to be a 6–7 range L.A. quake, which occurred on April 22, 1992. The second was to be a 7.8 L.A. quake, 150 miles east of L.A. and cause flooding. The second L.A. quake occurred June 28, 1992, 7.5 magnitude, 130 miles east of L.A., however no flooding occurred. The third earthquake in the Los Angeles area is to be in the range of an 8–9+ magnitude.[10]

Scallion went on to predict the next Los Angeles area quake in the time frame of July 25 to September 22, 1992. He said it would measure 8.3, plus or minus 0.5, with its epicenter within a 100-mile radius of Palm Springs. When it did not happen in that window, he later said that it only increases the probability that it would occur anytime between then (September 22, 1992) and May 8, 1993.

In the February 1993 issue, Scallion gave the final warning for super-mega quakes in California, 8–12 on the Richter scale. He said they would occur no later than May 9, 1993:

> As to the day and hour of the "big one" [California quake], this should not be seen as a singular event. While May of this year will be remembered as the month when the great plates shifted, events shall occur even before this—many [earthquakes] exceeding 7 on the Richter scale occurring roughly along a line drawn from Vancouver, B.C., to Eureka to San Diego. Think in terms of quakes lasting not seconds, but minutes! . . . The current Richter scale will not be able to measure its magnitude. Later it shall be computed to have been in excess of 10 and a new scale shall be created.[11]

When we move ahead to the April 1994 issue of Scallion's *Earth Changes Report*, Scallion says:

Everyone is still waiting for the Big One to occur. I have stated at my seminars and through ECR, that I do not see it happening this way. I see a "domino" series of Big Ones occurring over a period of five or more years, until the Isles of California are formed before the end of this century, perhaps before the end of '95 (see *The Future Map of the U.S: 1998–2001*). The March 20, 5.3 L.A. region earthquake has been classified by the U.S.G.S. as an aftershock of the Jan. 17 Northridge quake. I do not believe this to be the case. The epicenter of the March 20 quake was 40 miles east of Northridge and within the 50-mile perimeter of my predicted 8.3 Palm Springs-area quake. As stated previously in ECR, I believe the Jan. 17 Northridge quake has triggered and will trigger other faults known and unknown.[12]

Scallion's predictions, however, were not limited to California. According to David Sunfellow:

While western portions of the United States are being broken up, the eastern portions of America will also be undergoing major changes: Portions of New York will be inundated, Manhattan will lose approximately fifty percent of its land, one third or more of Maine's coast will be lost, most of Rhode Island will become submerged, more than half of Connecticut will go into the sea, Long Island will completely disappear, fifty percent of Florida will be inundated . . . the Midwest will also undergo major changes. Chief among these changes will be the Great Lakes expanding into one giant inland sea while the Mississippi River will expand into one gigantic seaway. . . . Alaska will lose about twenty-five percent of its land . . . only four of the Hawaiian Islands will be habitable after the changes—Kauai, Oahu, Maui, Hawaii—and these four will lose approximately twenty-five percent of their land. . . . Japan will be completely swallowed by the ocean. . . . Scallion believes the major changes listed above will be followed by a shift in the Earth's poles, which will take place sometime between 1998 and 2001.[13]

This, then, is a summary of the essence of the Earth change and prophecy information that I received during this period of my personal evolution. It doesn't leave much to say. Earth changes say it all.

But (read on), they say it with love.

Notes

1. Leonard Orr, *Physical Immortality: The Science of Everlasting Life* (Sierraville, CA: Inspiration University, 1980), p. 63.

2. Moira Timms, *Prophecies & Predictions: Everyone's Guide to the Coming Changes* (Santa Cruz, CA: Unity Press, 1980), p. 84 (citing *Newsweek*, Oct. 7, 1974, p. 57).

3. Ibid., pp. 84–86.

4. Quail Littlefield, "Science Affirms Hopi Prophecy for Sacred Lands" (Nevada City, CA: People Concerned for Mother Earth).

5. A translation of the oral traditions of the Hopi Prophecy given by Dan Katchongva, the late Sun Clan leader of Hotevilla. From the www web page entitled *From the Beginning of Life to the Day of Purification.*

6. JZ Knight, "Changes" (Yelm, WA: Ramtha Dialogues, 1986), video.

7. Gordon-Michael Scallion, *The Earth Changes Report* (Westmoreland, NH: Matrix Institute), volume 2.1, January 1, 1992, p. 5; article by Diana Leafe Christian, "California Earthquakes and Geophysical Changes 1992–1997."

8. Gordon-Michael Scallion, *The Earth Changes Report* (Westmoreland, NH: Matrix Institute), volume 2.4, May 1, 1992, p. 3.

9. Charles Petit, *Chronicle* Science Writer, San Francisco *Chronicle*, "Fault Caught in Act of Forming," July 3, 1992.

10. Gordon-Michael Scallion, *The Earth Changes Report*, issue no. 11, July 25, 1992, p. 1.

11. Gordon-Michael Scallion, *The Earth Changes Report* (Westmoreland, NH: Matrix Institute), issue no. 17, February 1993, p. 1.

12. Gordon-Michael Scallion, *The Earth Changes Report* (Westmoreland, NH: Matrix Institute), issue no. 31, April 1994, p. 8.

13. David Sunfellow, *Gordon-Michael Scallion: A Summary of His Most Important Predictions* (New Haven, CT: New Earth, 1995).

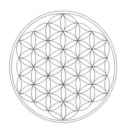

4

ACTIVATION

Now you know pretty much what I knew in July 1992. In fact, you know more. You know California did not fracture into the sea by May 9, 1993. You know too that it hasn't happened yet.

But you also know that Scallion must have been on to *something*. He did have an 87% accuracy rating. How many of you successfully predicted the October 17, 1989, Loma Prieta earthquake, or the Eureka quakes, or the two Los Angeles area quakes?

To further compound the issue, anything more than a superficial look at the environmental situation tells you that we are in *big* trouble elsewhere too.

In *Nothing*, I mentioned two of the ecological problems facing the Earth: the dying oceans and seas, and the destruction of the ozone layer. Now I will mention two more: underground nuclear testing and global warming.

I first heard about the serious consequences of the underground nuclear testing from Ramtha in 1986 in his "Changes" video. Then Drunvalo mentioned it in greater detail during his 1992 Flower of Life appearances. Drunvalo explained how the tremendous energy unleashed by such testing just rips apart tectonic plates, adding that the entire planet is on "Red Alert" as a result of this. Also, according to Adam

Trombley, we may be only a few bombs away from shattering the planet itself. The Indian Ocean has fallen more than twenty feet in some areas as a result of this testing.

The next problem, the greenhouse effect, is probably more closely related to global cooling than it is to global warming. Drunvalo, commenting on the research of John Hamaker,[1] said that ice ages progress according to a pattern of 90,000 years of ice followed by 10,000 years of warmth. We have just, by the way, had 10,000 years of warm weather. He also noted that ice ages are tied to the minerals: when the ice recedes, the rocks get ground up and the resulting minerals create fertile growing conditions that last for 10,000 years. Then the minerals are depleted and the trees begin to die. One acre of trees contains fifty tons of carbon dioxide, which is released into the air when the trees are cut, burned, or they die. This contributes to the greenhouse effect, which warms the oceans at the equator. Moisture-filled hot air then rises from the tropics and is carried to the poles, which increases the ice pack. The cold dry air then goes to the equator at low altitude, causing more moisture-filled hot air to rise, etc.

The time it takes to go from temperate weather to ice is twenty years. So we could be *very* close to another ice age that will last for 90,000 years!

Whether it is the oceans, the ozone layer, or the greenhouse effect, it should be obvious to everyone that something is happening on the planet, that these are not "normal" times. I get one hundred percent agreement on that in every lecture or workshop I give.

There are different ways of looking at this. Prophecies and the environmental situation are just two of them. Consider, for example, the incredible amounts of information we are gathering: the information collected by our civilization is increasing exponentially to the point where it is doubling every few years. We are on the verge of creating self-aware computers along with many other Star Trek-type advances in technology—"advances" that put us further out of spiritual balance and harmony with the Earth.

What Scallion is seeing are *likely* events preceding and ultimately leading to a pole shift—events that would *usually* happen at the end of a cycle. He seems to have a fourth-dimensional-type awareness that gives him a greater ability to perceive time both ways—future and past. This enables him to see events that almost certainly would happen. But something else is going on here.

Let me take you on a detour.

The idea of the Earth's poles shifting, by the way, is not new. Our governments have been aware of it and have been preparing for it probably since the 1950s.

Bill Cooper, in his book *Behold A Pale Horse*,[2] refers to a symposium held in 1957. The conclusion of its discussions was that the planet would self-destruct around the year 2000. Cooper says that this symposium came up with three recommendations for survival, called Alternatives One, Two, and Three.

Alternative One, according to Cooper, was to use nuclear devices to blast a hole in the stratosphere in order to let the heat and pollution escape (I never did understand that one). Also, it involved elevating human consciousness to the point where we could live in harmony with ourselves and our environment. This plan was quickly rejected as having little chance of being successful. I agree.

Alternative Two called for the construction of a series of deep underground bases and tunnels in which a few would be saved to carry on the human race. One of the earliest and perhaps the best known of the underground bases is the NORAD base located near Colorado Springs, Colorado. According to Richard Sauder, in his book *Underground Bases and Tunnels*,[3] planning for this 4.5-acre, fifteen-building complex began in 1956 and construction was started in 1961. We now have underground bases and tunnels extending into New Mexico and Arizona, and the largest one is not even in the United States. It is in Pine Gap, Australia.

One of the more interesting underground facilities is Mount Weather near Bluemont, Virginia. According to Sauder, it was constructed in the 1950s to house the United States government in the event of nuclear war. Mount Weather also allegedly houses a resident, back-up government.

The most well known of the Alternatives, Alternative Three, was about leaving the planet altogether and building a colony on Mars. This is discussed in a book and a video of the same name, and is detailed in "The Secret Government" chapter in *Nothing*.

In addition, in 1950, Canadian scientist David Suzuki and his team of researchers witnessed a spiraling light moving rapidly past the Earth. This highly unusual phenomenon was unknown in recorded human experience.

Further research revealed that this spiral of light was coming off the sun every three years, and increasing in intensity each time. It was also affecting a particular planetary motion, a wobble in the Earth's axis that is on a fourteen-year cycle.

In 1968, Suzuki published a paper that first went only to the Canadian government, then to the United States and most other governments, saying two things: (1) there would be an unparalleled explosion on the sun in August or September of 1972, and (2) the change in the fourteen-year wobble would lead to a pole shift by the winter of 1984.

Suzuki's warning was taken very seriously by the governments. Drunvalo says the Canadian government essentially gave him the facilities of the University of British Columbia (and anything else he wanted) to do his research. Drunvalo also said the Canadian government built huge underground spheres in the Rocky Mountains that would hold twenty-four humans (twelve males and twelve females).

These spheres were built to survive anything, including the ocean crashing into the mountains. In that event, quite likely during a pole shift, they would break out and float. Survivalists, both individuals and communities of people storing food and ammunition, sprang up in anticipation of the poles shifting. One such community, known as the Stelle Group, has been planning since 1972.

According to John White, in his book *Pole Shift*,[4] the Stelle Group is a self-sufficient community of approximately one hundred people on 240 acres of land located about sixty-five miles southeast of Chicago. It has several dozen homes, a water treatment facility, a small market, a sewer system, as well as a plastics and woodworking business.

The Stelle Group believes they know exactly when the poles will shift: May 5 in the year 2000. On that date the planets in our solar system will be aligned in such a way as to produce a much greater gravitational effect than usual. They believe that this will trigger the shift.

Richard Noone is another proponent of the potential disaster from this planetary alignment, when Saturn, Jupiter, and Mars will align on one side of the sun, with Venus, Mercury, and our moon in front of the Earth, all forming a straight (almost) line. It is likely that this alignment will exert far more gravitational pull than the alignment that occurred in 1982 and create greater potential for disaster. A key component in Noone's theory regarding the May 5, 2000, planetary alignment is the ice build-up at the South Pole. It is at least two and a half miles thick, and it is forming off-center at an alarming rate (two and one half billion tons of new ice every day). He seems to think that the planetary alignment will be the trigger, upsetting the Earth's axis and sending ice and water all over the Earth's surface.[5]

In addition to the ice build-up, there are active volcanoes underneath the ice with flowing rivers. A chunk of ice about the size of Rhode Island recently broke off Antarctica.[6]

Another factor to add to the mix is an unsteady sway in the Earth's axis, the Chandler Wobble, which operates similarly to a spinning top slowing down. This vacillation is increasing, and we all know what a top does when this happens. The Chandler Wobble is in addition to the fourteen-year wobble that captured the attention of David Suzuki, which is also slowing down.

A theory proposed by Swedish physicist Hannes Alvenis—magnetohydrodynamics or MHD—attempts to explain how a pole shift might express itself. This theory states that beneath the Earth's solid crust is a layer of rock that under normal conditions is solid. However, if the Earth's magnetic field collapses, as it does when the poles shift, this layer of rock becomes a liquid allowing the Earth's crust to shift position. A replica of this event has been demonstrated in laboratories.

By the way, the 1957 symposium discussed in Bill Cooper's book mentioned nothing of pole shifts. They were talking about another "single greatest problem" on the planet today—overpopulation—and how civilization as we know it would collapse around the year 2000 unless drastic steps were taken to curb population growth.

There are two ways the Earth's population can be reduced. Either you reduce the birth rate, or you increase the death rate. Cooper tells of several programs that have been used to reduce the birth rate, including birth control, and medical procedures such as sterilization, abortion, and hysterectomies. He also said that since these measures have been largely ineffective, "the only alternative left to the world's ruling elite was to increase the death rate."[7]

According to Cooper:

> Several Top Secret recommendations were made by Dr. Aurelio Peccei of the Club of Rome. He advocated that a plague be introduced that would have the same effect

as the famous Black Death of history. The chief rec-
ommendation was to develop a microbe which would
attack the auto-immune system and thus render the
development of a vaccine impossible. The orders were
given to develop the microbe and to develop a prophylactic and a cure. The microbe would be used against
the general population and would be introduced by vaccine. The prophylactic was to be used by the ruling elite.
The cure will be administered to the survivors when it
is decided that enough people have died. The cure will
be announced as newly developed when in fact it has
existed from the beginning. This plan is a part of Global
2000. The prophylactic and the cure are suppressed.[8]

Cooper went on to say that "undesirable" elements of
society were targeted, specifically the Black, Hispanic, and
homosexual populations. He said, "The African continent
was infected via smallpox vaccine in 1977. The vaccine was
administered by the World Health Organization. . . . The U.S.
population was infected in 1978 with the hepatitis B vaccine
. . . conducted by the Centers for Disease Control in New
York, San Francisco, and four other American cities. . . . The
gay population was infected. The ads for participants specifically asked for promiscuous homosexual male volunteers.
Whatever causes AIDS was in the vaccine."[9] Cooper said
this order was given by the Policy Committee of the Bilderberg Group.

According to Cooper, other measures to reduce population were ordered, such as the

> . . . Haig-Kissinger Depopulation Policy, which is
> administered by the State Department. This policy dic-
> tates that Third World nations take positive and effec-
> tive steps to decrease their populations and hold them
> in check or they get no aid from the United States. If

the Third World nations refuse, civil war usually breaks out and the rebels are usually found to be trained, armed, and financed by the Central Intelligence Agency. That is why many more civilians (especially young fertile females) than soldiers have been killed in El Salvador, Nicaragua, and other places. . . . The Haig-Kissinger depopulation policy has taken over various levels of government and is in fact determining U.S. foreign policy. The planning organization operates outside the White House and directs its entire efforts to reduce the world's population by 2 billion people through war, famine, disease, and any other means necessary.[10]

If you find this information somewhat unsettling, you now know how I felt in the months following my discovery of it. I remember in August 1992, going to an Oakland A's game with a friend I hadn't seen for a while. The Chicago White Sox were in town, and given that my friend is a Chicago native, it served as an appropriate reunion. Stu had put up with my "weirdness" for many years, but this particular outing was too much even for him. The evening ended with my giving him copies of all of Scallion's newsletters. It also ended with my knowing I would probably never see him again.

Even though I had met Drunvalo through his Flower of Life videos in June 1992 and had been presented with the larger picture by him, the information had not yet integrated for me—in fact, it was during that time period when I had one foot out of the state. I was seriously considering vacating California. I recall in the spring of 1993 (sometime before May 8) talking to Drunvalo on the telephone. He told me he was giving a workshop in Southern California, somewhere in the desert, in the summer of that year. That gave me a bold chance to take my head out of the sand. I also thought, "If he thinks it's safe, maybe it is."

That's when things first began to integrate for me. Soon I let go of the idea of leaving California. I was also letting go of the idea that Scallion's predictions had to happen.

So if you do feel unsettled, please note that there is a greater reality. I will lay that out in the next chapter, but only so it can serve as a foundation for what this book is really about. I will just say here that there is a bigger picture and that you are involved in the process—the process of moving through your fears and limitations so that you can step into the real drama of our time and more fully participate.

Notes

1. John Hamaker, *The Survival of Civilization* (Seymour, MO: Hamaker-Weaver, 1982).

2. Milton William Cooper, *Behold A Pale Horse* (Sedona, AZ: Light Technology Publishing, 1991).

3. Richard Sauder, Ph.D., *Underground Bases and Tunnels: What is the government trying to hide?* (Abingdon, VA: Dracon Press, 1995).

4. John White, *Pole Shift* (Virginia Beach, VA: A.R.E. Press, 1980).

5. "Enter Darkness, Enter Light: Can We Change our Predicted Doom?" (Glencoe, IL: New Millennium Productions, 1994), video.

6. Helmut Rott, Pedro Skvarca, Thomas Nagler, "Rapid Collapse of Northern Larsen Ice Shelf, Antarctica," *Science* magazine, vol. 271, Feb. 9, 1996, p. 788.

7. Milton William Cooper, *Behold A Pale Horse* (Sedona, AZ: Light Technology Publishing, 1991), p. 167.

8. Ibid., p. 167.

9. Ibid., p. 168.

10. Ibid., p. 169.

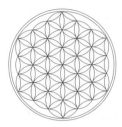

5

RESOLUTION

The last two chapters were probably not easy for you to read; they certainly were not easy for me to write! But I do believe it is necessary to have some degree of awareness of what is happening on planetary levels.

I have mentioned a bigger picture. This book is about stepping into and living that bigger picture. Because everything is a function of consciousness, all the problems I have thus far mentioned, like all problems, can be solved by raising our consciousness.

One of the keys to raising your consciousness is learning to move *through* your fears and limitations. That doesn't come by avoiding them or denying them. Moving through them leads to something I call integration, which is the inevitable result of an all-inclusive, both-eyes-open approach. Integration is one of the main themes of this book.

The integrative seeds were planted for me in June 1992 when I met Drunvalo via the Flower of Life. There was no formal workshop—it was just a group, about fifteen to twenty of us, who gathered to watch the videos. I recall sitting in the back of a fairly long, rectangular conference room. I was too far away to see much on the TV, but I could hear, and what I was hearing was wise. I was instantly impressed with

Drunvalo; he was obviously the possessor of great knowledge, and he was presenting it in such a sincere, innocent, and humble way. He didn't have anything extra going on with it. He definitely wasn't trying to prove anything or convince anyone.

In addition, his material was all-inclusive—he was talking about Earth changes, the environmental problems, the Greys, the secret government—all in the context of the bigger picture. He was in full possession of an awareness that something bigger than all of this was going on, and over the course of thirty-two hours, he slowly let it unfold.

It was this broad approach that impressed me the most. I had known for a long time the principles of integration—that it can come only from expanding to include *all* of what is going on, including the parts that you would tend to avoid or deny. I had learned not to pay much attention to people who claimed they had the "answer" but did not understand this most basic and important point.

So what is the bigger picture? To begin, there are two specific movements which our planet makes. We must understand both of these in order for any of this to make sense. First, we and our entire solar system revolve through space in a manner that indicates we are attached to another celestial body. We are as connected to the star Sirius as we are to the moon or the sun. The ancient Egyptians recognized this and aligned the temples along the Nile to the heliacal rising of Sirius—on July 23 of every year, in the east, one minute before the sun. The Great Pyramid is likewise aligned to this spot. The eyeballs of the Sphinx are looking right at it.

The other motion is the precession of the equinoxes (Fig. 5-1). The Earth's spin axis, in addition to being tilted $23\frac{1}{2}$ degrees, wobbles. This change in position causes the equinoctial points to regress one degree every seventy-two years; it changes the viewpoint of one zodiacal constellation every 2160 years, making one complete revolution every 25,920

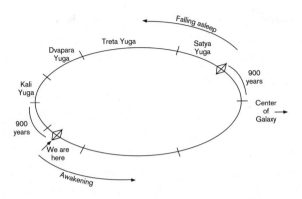

Figure 5–1. The precession of the equinoxes.

years. Seen from the North Pole, the axis traces an ellipse. At "perigee" on this ellipse we are closest to the center of the galaxy; at "apogee," we are farthest away and moving in a counter-clockwise direction. Our consciousness is directly related to this aeonic movement. As we move toward the center of the galaxy we wake up; as we move away from the center we fall asleep. From a tiny wobble we literally shift dimensional levels, stepping not only into brand new worlds but also into a completely different way of interpreting the one reality. Simultaneously, great physical changes occur, no less than the poles shifting, i.e., the planet turns over in space.

It is not at the two points closest and farthest from the center of the galaxy where this shift happens, but rather at two points nine hundred years removed from each of them.

As we approach these zones of change, we reach environmental maximums on all kinds of levels, even as we are now. Why? Because we are 180 degrees opposite the time when the poles and our consciousness last shifted. We are in the midst of great changes and are about to experience changes greater than our ability to imagine.

Many people interpret these changes metaphorically. For example, on a radio program where I was recently interviewed, one caller had his own version of California falling into the ocean, saying that it had already happened: in 1964 Esalen Institute opened and California did fall into the ocean—the ocean of emotions—and it started a revolution towards the light. He also had his own interpretation of Edgar Cayce's prediction of the destruction of New York. "What is New York?" he asked. "It is the financial center of the world. This means the end of the material world will come to pass. We are going towards the light with this whole evolution of consciousness. People have to think of these things as metaphors."

Another individual (whom I'll call David) sees the upcoming pole shift as a polarity shift, a balancing of the masculine and the feminine principles—much-overdue balancing, by the way. He understands it as a metaphor for profound internal changes. The masculine or left-brain in all of us, the part that sees itself as separate from and trying to control Nature and life, is being balanced by the feminine or right-brain, the side in all of us that is able to intuit the oneness of all life.

David believes the Earth is already in the fourth dimension and that humanity is fluctuating between the third and fourth dimensions. He sees the third dimension as a high-level dense place where fear, duality, and separation appear to be real. As we move up in vibration, these elements begin to dissolve—first on an inner level and then on an outer one. This is extraordinary, as he sees it, because the whole socio-economic system—the medical military industrial complex, as he calls it—is a fear-based system. It is based on keeping people disempowered—that's how they control us. Since we have bought into it, we have simultaneously accepted a very limited conception of who we are. That is all changing. As it changes, we are stepping into our birthright of health, peace, and freedom. We begin to identify much more closely with our true nature.

Except for the fact that we are not yet in the fourth dimension, I am in complete agreement with all of these points—

and I see the upcoming shifts literally, that we really will switch dimensional levels into a shorter wavelength where the reality is completely different, and that the poles will shift at the same time. I also see that these events are directly related to our consciousness. If we approach these changes in fear, then we will literally create a fearful experience, a cataclysm. If we can raise our consciousness to the point where we can attune to these events, they will be a beautiful experience, a different kind of cataclysm. Since it is not helpful in any way to approach the coming shift with fear, we must find a way to integrate any fears we may have about the coming changes. That will be my focus throughout the rest of this book.

But I want to further complete the big picture. Gordon-Michael Scallion is seeing likely events preceding and leading up to the poles shifting—events that would usually happen as we approach the end of a cycle. But something else is going on.

In *Nothing*, I explained in detail how the Sirians intervened in David Suzuki's predicted crisis in 1972 by creating a holographic protection field around the Earth. Their objective was threefold: (1) to protect us from the sun's pulse; (2) to do it without our knowledge and; (3) to speed up our evolutionary process to get us to the point where we could protect ourselves.

The third point is the key here. Their original intention was just to give us a little push, but that push never stopped. We have continued to accelerate to the point where it has gotten ridiculous.

What this means in part is that we are already in a different reality. Events that would normally happen may not happen that way at all. It means that our thoughts, feelings, and actions are more powerful than ever, and we have the ability to instantly alter our reality. This is why the success rate of many predictions (Cayce, Nostradamus, etc.) has fallen off dramatically since 1972.

It also means that we on Earth have the attention of all life everywhere in the universe. Life has never, anywhere, seen anything like this. Just the mere fact that they are watching us has a direct impact. Science knows that the observer affects the outcome of the experiment. But they are not just observing. Higher life forms are coming here to participate directly. They are doing this both as walk-ins and through birth.

So, even though destiny looks as positive as it does negative, the ascended masters don't know the outcome for sure. If we buy into mass negativity, it could get very ugly. Their belief is that we are in a mass dream and if we wake up to that reality, we can create it any way we want it. In an ideal scenario we will all ascend as one, as though we were a million years advanced in our evolution.

The usual scenario leading up to the shift is massive breakdown of all systems with total chaos and confusion. This time, however, we have an opportunity to keep it all together right up to the shift. It could happen very suddenly with almost no warning. It also could be an incredibly beautiful experience.

This leads to the most important task of all—doing the necessary inner work. Since our thoughts, feelings, and actions are creating our reality unerringly, and since they are more powerful than ever, our responsibility is to raise the quality of our thoughts and feelings so that they are in harmony with life—so that our personal reality mirrors universal reality. We must step consciously into the reality that this *is* a mass dream, learn to act in unison, and see and feel with one hundred percent intention what we want.

Do we want to live out of fear and ignorance, or do we want to create heaven on Earth? The choice is ours.

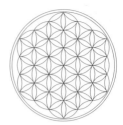

6

THE SECRET GOVERNMENT

In the chapter on the secret government in my first book, I stated the following: Whether you call them the secret government, the Illuminati, the Bilderbergers, the Trilateral Commission, or the Council on Foreign Relations, the name is irrelevant. The "secret government" is basically made up of the richest people in the world. There are about two thousand of them and they have been controlling our so-called governments for a long time. They control who gets elected, when, and where; they control when there is a war and when there isn't. They control planetary food shortages and whether a country's currency is inflated or deflated. All these things are dominated completely by these people. They can't control natural disasters, of course, but they can and do control a lot.[1] Now just what do I mean by that?

First, let's give a little background. I initially heard of the secret government in January 1991 when Doug gave me a copy of Bill Cooper's manuscript "The Secret Government: The Origin, Identity, and Purpose of MJ-12."[2] Shortly thereafter I discovered his book *Behold A Pale Horse*.[3] Prior to that, I always sensed there was something going on behind the scenes. The events of the 1960s caused me to wake up a great deal—both Kennedy assassinations, the assassination of Martin Luther King, Jr., and of course, Vietnam. But really I had no idea what was going on. Cooper's information was a great awakening for me, to say the least.

In June 1992, Drunvalo gave detailed information about the secret government, but with one *big* difference. He was speaking from the context of the bigger picture, that we need to wake up and move into the reality of oneness; they are us and we are them—we are all in this together. He also pointed out that these people operate almost totally from the left brain, that they are extremely intelligent—and they have almost no emotional bodies.

He went on to say that any of us would probably act pretty much in the same way if we had no emotions. Power and control are about all that is left.

More recently, I discovered an even better source of information on the secret government, David Icke's book ... *and the truth shall set you free.*[4] Then as luck would have it (it was pure luck, of course), Icke happened to be in the Bay Area, so I went to hear him speak and I came home with a copy of his video *Turning of the Tide....*[5]

Icke has not only done his homework, but he has a grasp of spiritual context. This combination makes him an excellent source.

What follows is a summary of the research I have done regarding the secret government. To begin, Icke says we need to understand that the pyramid is the basic structure of society, whether secret societies, governments, banks, corporations, or universities. That means there are a very few people at the top of the pyramid who know the full story. The closer you get to the base, the less is known. This is called compartmentalization. Most people are informed only on a "need to know" basis. The people at the bottom may know very little of the true nature of their organization.

The intelligence agency network, the banking system, the multinational corporations, the global media network, and so on, are all pyramids.

Then, according to Icke's video:

> There is a global pyramid within which all these work, in which the peaks of all these individual pyramids— banking, business, media, etc., fuse into one peak. Up there it is speculated by many that there are thirteen families at the peak. Percolating down through these different levels is the same basic policy, which is pushing the world towards more and more centralization of power.
>
> Within this global pyramid are a series of organizations which working together form the core of the secret government of the world.[6]

Icke says that the goal of this secret government is a one-world government with centralized control including: a central bank to administer all financial transactions in an electronic cashless society, a world army, and a micro-chipped population linked to a global computer.

Icke goes on to say how this is all operating well above the level of the outer governments; that in fact those at the top of the pyramid manipulate events to make sure *their* people get into positions of power. FDR once said, "In politics nothing happens by accident; if it happens you can bet it was planned that way."[7]

According to Icke, this whole scenario is played out by the politicians and the media as though presidents and prime ministers are at the top of the decision-making process. According to media portrayals, the ones above the visible political leaders who really make the decisions don't even exist. (No doubt most journalists are unaware of this secret government anyway.) Yet these elites are the ones who run and control it all—the money, the media, and even who is *allowed* to run for high office.

Icke goes on to tell how this group of organizations began after the establishment of a secret society in Britain known as the Round Table. He says that in 1919 the American members of this secret society met with the British members and they decided to create off-shoot organizations, which, working together, would constitute a major part of the secret government of the world.

The Royal Institute of International Affairs (RIIA) was the first of these off-shoot organizations. It was founded in 1920 in London. Then in 1921 came its American counterpart, the Council on Foreign Relations (CFR).

Icke says that the RIIA and the CFR both work behind the scenes to control foreign policy, although they affect other policies also. It should be noted that since 1921, virtually all U.S. presidents have been CFR members. Since FDR, they all have, with one exception—JFK.

In 1954 came the key organization, the Bilderberg Group. Its members include the top people in politics, banking, multinational corporations, the military, and the media.

Then in 1972–73, the Trilateral Commission was created by David Rockefeller (a CFR and Bilderberg member) and Zbigniew Brzezinski. Its purpose was to coordinate the control pattern among Europe, the United States, and Japan. One of its first goals was to elect one of its members to the United States Presidency. This was accomplished in 1976 when Jimmy Carter, who ran as an "outsider," was elected. Of course, his Cabinet was awash with CFR and Trilateralists including Zbigniew Brzezinski, Carter's national security advisor. Icke says that this has continued to be the case with every succeeding administration.

So why don't we ever hear about these organizations and their agendas? The closest the media ever comes to including them is an occasional reference to them as "think tanks." Likely the answer has to do with the fact that the media is controlled or owned by members of these organizations.

Now let's look at the 1992 presidential election. On the surface, it looked as though there might be a choice, like there might actually be some differences between the candidates. But a closer examination shows us that the choice was between Republican George Bush, who is a member of the Council on Foreign Relations, the Trilateral Commission, and the Skull and Bones Society; and Democrat Bill Clinton, who is a member of the Council on Foreign Relations, the Trilateral Commission, and the Bilderberg Group. Are you getting the picture?

On the surface, there are supposed great differences between the two parties, yet the presidential candidates for either party are hand-picked by secret government organizations.

Nothing happens on this level unless it is allowed to happen.

Furthermore, the President's inner circle is composed solely of members of these organizations. That means in order even to be considered for a Cabinet position, or a key ambassadorship, you must be an insider, a member of one of these organizations.

Consider also how the secret government controls war situations. When you own both sides, you can't lose. You spawn the conditions that lead to war, then you manipulate behind the scenes to control who wins, then you offer the "solution" to the problem. Of course, since you created the problem in the first place, the solution is predesigned to tighten your rein on the controls.

After World War I we were given the League of Nations as the "solution." It failed, so conditions were created that

made World War II inevitable. Its solution was the United
Nations. The "solution" in each case is moving us increasingly closer to the New World Order, the One World Government, with guess who at the helm.

They control whether a country's currency is inflated or
deflated via a central banking system. Consider the Federal
Reserve—that it is no more federal than Federal Express—
it is a private corporation, a "gift" given to us by the international bankers for the purpose of manipulating our
economy and our country. Consider the statement of Baron
M. A. Rothschild: "Give me control over a nation's currency
and I care not who makes its laws."[8]

According to the video "Liberty in the Balance":

> The initial argument in favor of central control of the
> money supply hinged on the potential ability of a cen-
> tral bank to maintain stability in the economy. Yet, since
> the Federal Reserve Act of 1913, we have had the stock
> market crash of 1929, the Great Depression, nine reces-
> sions, and the debt has risen from about one billion dol-
> lars to over four trillion dollars![9]

When I first heard of these things back in January 1991,
I tried to check it out as best I could. I decided to research
the Kennedy assassination. In case you haven't already figured it out, Lee Harvey Oswald did not kill JFK; he almost
certainly didn't even fire one shot. So if not Oswald, who?

For starters, consider how Kennedy, in his effort to control the national debt, was bypassing the Federal Reserve.
Instead of issuing Federal Reserve notes, he began printing debt-free United States notes. It is clearly indicated in
the U.S. Constitution that the Treasury Department has the
right to do this, yet in reality it is about the biggest NO there
is! That alone was enough to get him killed. The last pres-

ident to do this was Abraham Lincoln, and I'm sure you remember what happened to him. After the Kennedy assassination, Lyndon Johnson quietly went back to Federal Reserve notes.

Consider also Kennedy's deteriorating relationship with the CIA after the failed Bay of Pigs invasion, how he fired CIA director Allen Dulles and threatened "to splinter the CIA in a thousand pieces and scatter it to the winds."[10] Dulles was fired along with three others. One of the victims, General Charles P. Cabell, happened to have a brother in Dallas. His name was Earle Cabell; he was the mayor. Consider that the parade route was changed just that morning to allow the caravan to pass by the Texas School Book Depository and to make a turn of greater than one hundred degrees, which slowed it down to 10–12 miles per hour, thus creating a sitting-duck situation. Consider also that Allen Dulles was later appointed to the Warren Commission.

Kennedy was going against the global power structure in Vietnam. This was a war he was supposed to fight for many reasons. Yet he was withdrawing from Vietnam to the tune of one thousand soldiers a month. At the time of his death there were 16,000 "advisors" in Vietnam. His plan was to wait until after the next election, then in sixteen months to get completely out. Three days after the assassination Lyndon Johnson quietly rescinded Kennedy's directive. The Vietnam buildup began in earnest shortly after the 1964 election.

The Kennedy administration also declared war on organized crime, and when you consider the inner connection among the Mafia, the CIA, and Cuba, you realize that this was a definite no-no.

Bill Cooper asserts that Kennedy had discovered portions of truth with respect to both the presence of aliens and the drug situation in the United States. The ruling elite had cornered the drug market as a means of funding their "black" projects. According to Cooper:

> He issued an ultimatum in 1963 to Majesty Twelve. President Kennedy assured them that if they did not clean up the drug problem, he would. He informed Majesty Twelve that he intended to reveal the presence of aliens to the American people within the following year, and ordered a plan developed to implement his decision . . . .
>
> President Kennedy's decision struck fear into the hearts of those in charge. His assassination was ordered by the Policy Committee of the Bilderberg Group and the order was carried out by agents in Dallas.[11]

Ten days before his death, Kennedy spoke these startling words at Columbia University: "The high office of President has been used to foment a plot against the American people. Before I leave office, I must inform the citizen of his plight."[12]

Cooper also says that the fatal shot (not the only shot, but the fatal one) was fired by the driver of Kennedy's car, secret service agent William Greer. What is known for certain is that instead of putting his foot on the accelerator to get Kennedy out of danger (the way secret service agents are trained to do), Greer put on the brakes! Cooper says Greer had a pistol in his left hand and he turned and fired over his right shoulder. All eyewitnesses to this event seem subsequently to have come to an untimely death.

So this is the way "they" have been doing it.

Back to Alternative Three: After the so-called secret government completed their colony on Mars, as I indicated in *Nothing*, they made a shocking discovery—that the poles would be shifting on all the planets, including Mars.

The Greys never told them this, they just sat back and watched, knowing full well the project was a complete waste of time. This is the way of beings who have no emotional body. They looked at the people in the secret government just as the secret government has looked at us—like creatures of no more importance than bugs.

The Greys didn't tell the secret government elite the real situation, that what is really going on is an inter-dimensional shift. By 2012, the whole octave is going to shift up. Remember, there is voidness between each of the dimensional levels, and there is an even greater voidness between octaves. Drunvalo says it was created that way intentionally in order to keep out anyone not ready to enter. That means by 2012 we all have to go through the great, great void and into the next octave. And you cannot take anything with you, i.e., you cannot take any external machinery through, no UFOs! You can only go through as Spirit in complete Oneness to God and all life.

To their astonishment (and dismay) the secret government realized that they cannot separate themselves from us, that they cannot make it through the dimensional shift without us, that we are totally interlinked, and either we all make it or none of us do. This presented a big problem for such a left-brain culture.

But, after the shock wore off, they did what any good left-brained culture would do and began acting in a very logical manner towards that goal. They set in motion conditions that soon had communism and the Soviet Union collapsing and the Berlin Wall falling. These things didn't just "happen." They happened because they were *allowed* to happen.

It is important for us to come out of judgment on this so we can begin to see the bigger picture. I am always asked about the secret government in my Flower of Life workshops, and I am frequently asked about the Kennedy assassination. People become quite activated when hearing this information, and I am often asked how I can present it in an integrated way. The answer is that it has not always been that way for me. I have certainly gone through my outrage and disbelief. The JFK assassination was particularly difficult. I liked him; I trusted him; I felt he was really trying to do the right thing. When he died, a piece of me died too. When I discovered the truth about his assassination I was rather upset. It took a lot to integrate that, but the point is *I did integrate it*.

And that is something we all have to do. It can come only from a both-eyes-open approach, from expanding to include *all* of what is going on. We need to be aware of the "dark side" elements in the world, but we also need to be aware that they are us, that we cannot separate ourselves from them and pretend they are outside of us.

I repeat: We need to understand that whether they are "inside" or "outside" of us, they are still us. You cannot separate yourself from the whole. Whatever is going on "out there" is nothing but an external projection of what is going on inside each of us. We cannot heal our own personal lives until we expand to include, and come to terms with, our inner dark sides. The same is true out there.

We are all in this together, and we have re-created the same situation as that of Atlantis 16,000 years ago. At that time the Martians tried to split from the rest of Earth and go their own way. It didn't work then and it won't work now. We must become aware of ourselves as inseparable from the whole, that the only answer is unity. It is all of us or none of us!

I am also often asked if I feel safe talking about this. I do. First, going public is a matter of timing. Drunvalo was told by his angels that he had to wait until the timing was right. Had he presented this information before then, he probably would not have made it across the street. His timing coincided with the secret government's discovery of the true nature of events. Prior to that time, they were getting rid of anyone who was in their way. Since that time, they have been leaving people alone, even helping them if they think they might have an answer. Drunvalo was offered ten million dollars by the CIA. He refused it. I work with Drunvalo. I am part of the solution, a solution that includes *everyone*.

Drunvalo has told how he attracted the attention of the dark forces after an initiation in Egypt. In fact, the interest was so great that he attracted the attention of Lucifer himself!

So the two met face to face. Drunvalo's only instructions from Thoth were to stay in his protective, self-generated merkaba field and to tell the truth. Lucifer wanted to know what was going on; being Lucifer he suspected it was a continuation of the "many are called, few are chosen" scenario, the one where the "good guys" go through and the "bad guys" stay behind. Drunvalo told him that the plan was different this time, that it was to include *everyone*, with none excluded. Lucifer thought about it and then said very forcefully, "If that is true, I will leave you alone."

He has kept his word. Drunvalo has been allowed to proceed, because he is looking for an answer that includes everyone. So am I.

Another aspect of this had been puzzling to me. Even though the secret government had seen the bigger picture, it never seemed to me as though they were acting as one in preparing themselves, and the rest of us, for the upcoming shift.

For example, I learned in the winter 1995 issue of *The Montauk Pulse*[13] about the efforts of the operators of the Montauk Project to preserve the Earth's magnetic field. On the surface, this would seem like a noble idea. Our memories as well as our emotional bodies are tied to the magnetic field. If this field goes to zero and you have no protection (i.e., no merkaba field), you lose your memory! In addition you will find yourself in a brand-new dimensional world. This is exactly what happened to many of the survivors of Atlantis when the last dimensional shift occurred 13,000 years ago. These people were reduced to basic survival, learning to build a fire for warmth, and so on. They remained that way for more than six thousand years, until 4000 BC when the ascended masters started to give the lost knowledge back. Civilization as we know it began at that time.

So, superficially, trying to preserve the Earth's magnetic field might seem like a heroic effort, but perhaps the real motivation has more to do with keeping us in the third dimension, where the elite are able to maintain their power base.

Additionally, I learned from Drunvalo in an interview in the November/December 1996 issue of *Leading Edge Newspaper* the real motivation behind the French nuclear testing in late 1995 and early 1996. First, it wasn't just the French; several governments were involved. Drunvalo said the secret government wanted to blow up the axis of the Christ-consciousness grid. The axis of the Christ-consciousness grid runs from a point near the Great Pyramid in Egypt through the Earth and comes out on the other side in Maraya, a small island near Tahiti. This is very near where the French did their nuclear testing. Drunvalo said the plan was to detonate eight nuclear bombs, but that the "shaking" from the sixth blast woke Mother Earth from her state of unconsciousness from the last pole shift 13,000 years ago. Drunvalo said the Christ-consciousness grid was not damaged, and "on the sixth bomb they had their intelligence people inside the pyramids watching to see what would happen. At that moment a man appeared out of nowhere in the middle of them. He was one of the ascended masters. He didn't say a word. He opened up an etheric book and let them read

from it. After that they changed their minds and have can-
celed the other two bombings."[14]

In the same interview, Drunvalo talked about the HAARP
project (High-Frequency Active Auroral Research Program)
in Alaska. It was scheduled to go on-line in the spring of 1997
and "it's a weapon thousands of times stronger than an atomic
bomb . . . they can go into a country, like England, and destroy
the entire country in a matter of seconds once it is perfected."
He said it can also be used to change the weather and to control human moods, and that when it is fully turned on, they
really don't know what will happen—"They could actually
destroy the whole ionosphere! They don't know, but they're
willing to take the chance."[15]

In an earlier *Leading Edge* interview conducted on
December 22, 1995, Drunvalo said:

> They are not going to stop trying to do everything they
> can to try to control the whole situation. They are schiz-
> ophrenic right now. They are setting off nuclear devices
> at the same time others in the same group are prepar-
> ing for planetary unity, knowing in truth that is where
> they have to go. There are still too many aspects within
> them that do not truly understand what we are going
> through. If the whole body of the elite understood, then
> they could drop all this stuff. We would know it instantly.
> There are too many of them that do not comprehend.
> To appease those that do not understand, the other half
> is letting them go on with this kind of activity.[16]

He continued to discuss this ongoing schizophrenia in the
November/December 1996 issue:

> LE: You're saying that some of the levels of the secret
> government want you to be successful, not the groups
> that have broken away from the main group.

Drunvalo: Yes, they realize that we're the only ones (that they know of) who hold an answer for them that they can see, and they want us to be successful. It's the higher levels of the military who are scared to death. The reason they are afraid is that they are there with their time machines standing at the edge of the Great Void. They can go into the past and the future through the understandings of the Montauk experiments and through their remote viewing (two different systems). And now, as they're looking into the Great Void they're being told they have to go in there. This is very real for them. They have located the Great Void and have sent people in there and they have never come back out. They're scared to death.

LE: They know that, somehow, you've got the answers to the Great Void.

Drunvalo: Yes. Some of the higher levels of the secret government know. It's the lower levels we're having problems with right now. So, if it's necessary we will walk into their machines and go into the Great Void [editor's note: protected by a MerKaBa] and come out, so they can see that it's okay . . . that life just doesn't disappear, and so they can have hope because we want everybody to be unharmed by this, even the military. We'll prove to them that it's okay. Whatever it takes.[17]

This perhaps explains in some way why it does not appear that the secret government is acting in unison. They too are a pyramid structure within a pyramid structure, and only those at the top know the full extent of what is really going on.

Notes

1. Bob Frissell, *Nothing in This Book Is True, But It's Exactly How Things Are* (Berkeley, CA: Frog, Ltd., 1994), p. 175.

2. Milton William Cooper, "The Secret Government: The Origin, Identity, and Purpose of MJ-12" (Huntington Beach, CA: Manuscript copyright 1989).

3. Milton William Cooper, *Behold A Pale Horse* (Sedona, AZ: Light Technology Publishing, 1991).

4. David Icke, *. . . and the truth shall set you free* (Isle of Wight, England: Bridge of Love Publications, 1995).

5. David Icke, *Turning of the Tide . . .* (London, England: Bridge of Love Publications), two-hour video.

6. Ibid.

7. Ted Gunderson & Anthony J. Hilder, "Reichstag '95: An American Holocaust" (Anchorage, AK: Harvester Tapes, America United 1995), video.

8. "Liberty in the Balance: America, the FED and the IRS" (Pasadena, CA: Mosaic Media, 1993), video.

9. Ibid.

10. Mark Lane, *Plausible Denial* (New York: Thunder's Mouth Press, 1991), p. 93, citing *The New York Times*, April 25, 1966.

11. Milton William Cooper, *Behold A Pale Horse*, p. 215.

12. George C. Andrews, *Extra-Terrestrial Friends and Foes* (Lilburn, GA: Illuminet Press, 1993), p. 289.

13. Peter Moon, *The Montauk Pulse* (Westbury, NY: Sky Books), Newsletter, Winter 1995, vol. 1, no. 9, "Drastic Efforts Underway to Preserve the Earth's Magnetic Field."

14. *Leading Edge Newspaper* (Pisgah Forest, NC: Kenneth and Dee Burke, Publishers), Nov/Dec 1996, Interview with Drunvalo Melchizedek: "4th Dimension is upon us."

15. Ibid.

16. *Leading Edge International Research Journal* (Yelm, WA: Kenneth and Dee Burke, Publishers), Issue No. 88, "Leading Edge Interviews Drunvalo Melchizedek," December 22, 1995.

17. *Leading Edge Newspaper*, Nov/Dec 1996, Interview with Drunvalo Melchizedek: "4th Dimension is upon us."

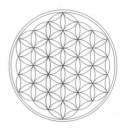

7

MAGNETIC FIELDS

Let me take you back to the story of the efforts of the Montauk Project to preserve the Earth's magnetic field. Preston Nichols, a key investigator of Montauk, discovered on a plane ride to tape a television show that he was sitting next to the current director of the Project. It was just a coincidence, of course.

Preston Nichols was one of the engineers in the earlier phases of Montauk, the event that on August 12, 1983, coupled with the Philadelphia Experiment of August 12, 1943. Preston is the co-author of *The Montauk Project: Experiments in Time*,[1] a book that gives a detailed description of the goings-on at Montauk. To briefly recap, Preston discovered at one point that he was living a dual life, one he was aware of, and one he wasn't. Through mind-manipulation techniques, he had been made completely unaware of his role in the Montauk Project—that is, until his memory blocks began to unravel and ultimately full awareness returned to him.

He and Peter Moon have co-authored four Montauk books; the first is the best, in my opinion. In it you will begin to understand the nature of our two-tiered technology system. There is technology we know about, and then there is a whole other technology you wouldn't believe. The Montauk

Project originally involved inter-dimensional time travel. Yes, you read that correctly. Al Bielek, who was involved in both the Philadelphia Experiment in 1943 and the Montauk Project in 1983, has said that with the Montauk technology—most of it coming from ETs—they could travel anywhere in the galaxy, and both ways in time, past and future. Not bad.

The main purpose of the August 12, 1983, part of the experiment was to connect with and try to correct the out-of-control external merkaba field in the Bermuda Triangle. This field is affecting the Earth as well as large areas of space. Its existence is the ongoing legacy of the Martians' failed experiment in Atlantis 16,000 years ago (see *Nothing*). Prior attempts to correct this situation were made in 1913 and 1943, and again in 1993. In each case the date was August 12, a day on which the biorhythms of the planet create conditions necessary to allow these experiments to take place.

According to Drunvalo, not only have these attempts all failed, but they have made the situation worse. He says the problem will be solved only on December 12, 2012. Somehow, on this date they will be able to get in there and correct the situation before the actual window of August 12, 2013.

What they are doing in the Montauk Project under the official title of the Phoenix Project is using merkaba fields—external ones, of course—for all sorts of purposes. Since the merkaba is the universal pattern of creation, a merkaba field can take any form you want it to.

Drunvalo says he met with Preston. In their discussion, Preston gave a detailed account of just how they were generating these fields. As a result, Drunvalo was convinced that Preston Nichols is who he says he is.

The Montauk Project later focused on mind control, for instance, during the Gulf War. The Iraqi soldiers had technology used on them that they couldn't possibly understand. They had no choice but to surrender en masse.

Anyway, back to the story. The current director of the Montauk Project, who identifies himself as Ken, told Preston of efforts underway to record the Akashic records of the Earth, which would give them a complete historical reading of the planet. They are doing this because they know the magnetic field is going to collapse, the loss of which will result not only in the loss of our individual memories, but also the loss of the Akashic records. (Author's note: I am only reporting to you from the article in *The Montauk Pulse;* however, my understanding is that the Akashic records *do* survive the collapse of the magnetic field and the resulting pole shift.)

Ken told Preston that the Akashic records are stored in the Van Allen belt, a doughnut-shaped high-intensity radiation belt which circles the Earth conforming to the Earth's magnetic field. He said thought forms coming from the Earth are stored there in miniature plasma doughnuts called plasmoids. He then said that they were erasing these plasmoids in a way that is enabling them to record the stored information. This will create a computer-style record of the Akashic records, which in turn will enable them to retain the Earth's memory when the magnetic field goes to zero.

Preston listened to this with interest, since he had known for some time that the Earth's magnetic field was decreasing. To quote directly from *The Montauk Pulse* newsletter:

> A further study showed there is a massive pulsing of a magnetic field that is being generated from Brookhaven Labs on Long Island. According to a worker, four very large cryogenic magnets have been placed within the confines of Brookhaven National Laboratory. This accounts for the pulsing of the magnetic field referred to above and also fits the theory that the "current director" of Montauk told Preston. A massive effort is being conducted to preserve the Earth's magnetic field.[2]

To understand why there is a massive effort to preserve the magnetic field we must turn to the November 7–11, 1996, Star Visions Conference in Estes Park, Colorado, where Drunvalo was a featured speaker. He opened with the following words:

> There are events happening in the world now that you need to know about . . . . there are certain governments that don't want you to know about them, they're doing everything they can to make sure you don't know about them, but it's important that you understand what's going on right now.

A space probe, *Ulysses*,[3] was sent to the sun by the European Space Agency and NASA. One of its missions was to measure the sun's magnetic field. It reached the apex of its flight over the south pole of the sun in September of 1994. Cosmic-ray physicists discovered, first as the craft measured the magnetic south pole, then the equator, and finally the magnetic north pole, that there was no measurable difference between the poles and the equator. This means that there is no longer a north and south pole on the sun. Whatever happens on the sun happens here!

Drunvalo then talked about the magnetic field of the Earth, how it first began to deteriorate about two thousand years ago, and how it dropped suddenly about five hundred years ago. About fifty years ago, the drop began to accelerate, and very recently it has *really* begun to fluctuate.

Drunvalo said that in September 1994 there were huge fluctuations. There were problems in landing airplanes, and that people were on an emotional roller coaster. He said it was very bad again between June and October of 1996, with the magnetic poles moving all over the place. According to Drunvalo, the magnetic south pole moved six hundred to one thousand miles from its standard site, and it even appeared off the coast of Los Angeles for a day. Magnetic maps are no longer good—birds who use the magnetic lines to migrate are ending up in the wrong places, and whales and dolphins are beaching themselves.

Drunvalo said that the South Pole has been shut down, that people there have become extremely unstable emotionally—killing each other and just generally going crazy. The FBI was sent there to investigate.

This is a phenomenon that is affecting everyone on the planet, dramatically. The closer you are to the South Pole, the more you will feel it. Remember our emotional stability as well as our memory are tied to the Earth's magnetic field.

Drunvalo also said that in November 1996, the field began to stabilize and that he didn't know if it was going to stop or continue. It is possible that we have less than two years before the shift! This could very well explain why there would seem to be this massive effort to preserve the Earth's magnetic field.

Drunvalo then talked about the Schumann Frequency, a wave form that comes out of the planet, the "heartbeat" of the Earth that has historically pulsed at a very specific frequency, 7.8 hertz. It has been so stable for so long that the military has used it to log in their instruments.

However, it has been increasing in the last few years and, according to author Gregg Braden, it had moved up to 8.6 hertz by 1994. In his book, *Awakening to Zero Point: The Collective Initiation*, he says:

> The net result of this increase is that each cell of your body is trying to match the rhythmic "heartbeat," or reference frequency, to that of Earth. Moving into the resonant pattern of a higher tone, each life form, including human, is attempting to map out a new rhythm, or "signature frequency."[4]

Gregg believes the shift will happen when this frequency reaches 13 hertz. Drunvalo says the frequency could be up to 11.2 hertz by now.

Now let's take a closer look at the significance of the changes in the magnetic field and how it is that our emotions and our memories are affected.

First, the normal occurrence as we approach the point in the precession of the equinoxes where change takes place is that everything begins to break down. This is because our emotional stability is directly tied to the magnetic field.

As the shift approaches, the magnetic field begins to greatly fluctuate over a three- to six-month period. This causes people to lose it emotionally, which in turn causes the economic and social structures to break down, because it is people who keep these structures together.

Drunvalo says that awareness of the dimensional shift has filtered down to the outer governments, and the FBI is very concerned about keeping the planetary peace as much as possible during the transition period.

Remember, our memory is also tied to the magnetic field. During the actual time of the dimensional shift, the three-and-one-half-day period when the magnetic field goes to zero, it is necessary to have some form of protection, like a merkaba, in order to consciously make it through.

In the absence of this protective field, we would most likely only make it to the third overtone of the fourth dimension, with our memories erased, just like when we die. We need the protection to continue consciously moving up, with our memory intact, to the tenth, eleventh, or twelfth overtone of the fourth dimension.

The chaos I described above is what usually happens, but it may well be different this time. We may be able to keep our emotional bodies relatively intact. If we can, we can create a much more gentle, organic, and conscious ride from one dimension to the next.

The point again is that it's all up to us. If we can consciously step into the realization that this is a mass dream, and we are the ones who are creating it, then we can create that gentle ride.

It all boils down to each one of us doing the necessary inner work.

Notes

1. Preston B. Nichols and Peter Moon, *The Montauk Project: Experiments In Time* (Westbury, NY: Sky Books, 1992).

2. Preston B. Nichols and Peter Moon, *The Montauk Pulse* newsletter (Westbury, NY: Sky Books), Winter 1995, vol. 1, no. 9.

3. Peter Aldhous, "Long-Awaited Probe Gets New View of the Sun," *Science* magazine (Washington, D.C.: American Association for the Advancement of Science), vol. 265, no. 5179, Sept. 16, 1994, p. 1659.

4. Gregg Braden, *Awakening to Zero Point: The Collective Initiation* (Questa, NM: Sacred Spaces/Ancient Wisdom, 1994), p.67.

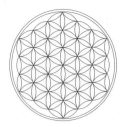

8

CHANGES

These tremendous Earth changes constitute a phenomenon that dramatically affects everyone on the planet. Just knowing this can help—sometimes a lot. Whenever you find yourself uncontrollably affected by your emotions, and especially if it includes interactions with others, pause for a moment and remind yourself of the Earth's changing magnetic field.

Drunvalo recommends putting a compass in a secure location where you know it will not move, so you can see for yourself how these fields are changing. He did it and has recorded an eight-and-one-half-degree shift from the compass needle's original position.

I too have placed a compass where I can easily check it. For about the first month I noticed no change. Suddenly there was a two-degree shift. If you do this, and you see changes like this, fasten your seat belt, because you will most likely be on an emotional roller coaster!

People everywhere are going through tremendous changes no matter what the magnetic field is doing. This is so because of where we are in the cycle of the precession of the equinoxes. We are in a time of major change, and the magnetic field is only one aspect of this.

In the process of writing this book I wondered how to explain what this means to each of us as individuals, and then God intervened directly and showed me exactly how to do it—in a way that was fun, easy, and, I believe, highly effective. I decided to present the information as the actual situation of a friend.

I came home one day (after a hard day of working on this book in the woods) to find a message on my answering machine from a friend, Brian Hall. I had put out a feeler to him earlier, wondering if he would be interested in a video exchange. He responded with an enthusiastic "yes" and then told me how anxious he was to talk to me, that there was a UFO convention coming up in August featuring the likes of Zecharia Sitchin, Richard Noone, David Icke, and Drunvalo, among others. He explained the theme of the convention was "The Hidden Human History" and the suppression and control of people and information.

I called him back to say that his message was very interesting, that the conference would be exploring some of the very themes I am writing about in this book. I then asked him, since this "coincidence" was just too good, if he had been digging through my garbage. His response was, "No, I'm sorting through my own garbage." He proceeded to talk about the many emotional changes he has been going through in a way that was exactly the message I wanted to convey in this chapter.

So we made an appointment to exchange videos. I asked if he would like to go for a hike and talk about all this on tape so that I might be able to use it in this chapter. He agreed.

I first met Brian in November 1995 during a ninety-minute van ride from the Las Vegas airport to the site of the eight-day, fifth annual International UFO Congress. I was a featured speaker, and Brian was there to take it all in. Everyone in that van, including Brian, was a real character. The ride was pretty much a non-stop laugh, with UFO and "missing time" jokes flowing freely, very freely!

Then in April 1996, I got a letter from him. He said he had read my book, that it had sufficiently blown his mind, and he wanted to find out about the Flower of Life workshop. I sent him a flyer informing him of my upcoming workshop in May in San Francisco and he enrolled.

Brian came to that workshop with great enthusiasm and with a tremendous thirst for the knowledge and information being imparted. He also brought the vast array of his own knowledge, along with a healthy dose of comic relief—always at the right moment. He took the Flower of Life workshop again in November. Both workshops were great; in fact, they were fantastic! Brian was a major contributor to the success of each.

What follows is the discussion we had on the day of our meeting on April 1, 1997.

Bob: What caught my attention about your phone call recently was that it concerned the exact themes I am writing about in *Something*. This includes the theme that when you step into the larger picture, when you begin to see clearly the many levels of reality, it puts you through some changes. That's really the central question I'm looking at in the book. One way I'm wording the question is: "In the context of these changes, including the dimensional shift, it's not useful to be in fear, yet how do you deal with the fear that all this new information and all these changes bring up for you?" Then you started talking about what all this is like for you. For example, who do you talk to? Many people will think you are a kook, and if you force-feed this to anyone you can easily lose friendships. Believe me, I know! You started sharing your personal saga at that point; you also expressed gratitude for having someone you could talk to who can relate to this sort of thing.

Brian: You do have that right, Bob. You are one of the few people who understands this. You've got to be grateful for the little things, including not only the association we've had with each other, with the Flower of Life, and Drunvalo, and the tape exchange, but also a growing friendship. You're a truly enlightened individual, so I am grateful to be able to exchange not only my observations, but also my feelings. Like you said, these changes we're going through have involved for me personally some pretty good highs and also some really deep lows. There have been nights—I don't understand it— some people would say, "Brian, you're acting like a little school kid," but I'll literally start crying at the drop of a hat. What is going on? There are nights when I ask "Why am I weeping for people and places that I know little about? Why do I weep for Third World countries? Why do I weep for my own pathetic little problems? Why do I weep for perhaps past-life energies that I'm still having to deal with and not really knowing how to deal with"—like you said, there is going to be that fear and some sadness . . . . I'm hoping I'm due a day of great joy, when I just run around and act like a kook without caring what other people think. I'm still stuck about what other people think—David Icke talked about that— we're so concerned about what others think that we're not being true to ourselves and it's hard to talk to people about that. It's also hard to talk to people about Earth changes, UFOs, the secret government, the Federal Reserve, and how we've literally been screwed by a global elite, whether people want to admit it or not.

Bob: You were talking about getting emotional. There is a two-pronged area here that I see. First, the magnetic field is fluctuating and our emotions are tied to it—that can explain a lot. But the question I'm more interested in is this: Do you wonder what is going on when you're in the middle of it; do you know how to deal with it, or not, and how do you interact with that? Can you first answer the question, do you know how to deal with it?

Brian: To be honest with you, I don't know how to deal with it. I've been in sort of an action-reaction mode—I respond and I don't understand why I'm responding. I'm responding, perhaps, to a lot of fear-based information and I need to work through that. How? I don't know. All I can really do is speak from personal experience. I guess it's just a waking-up process, if that's what you want to call it, realizing I'm being affected by the magnetic field, which I still don't really understand. But on a daily basis, one minute I will be fine, the next I will have what I call a mortality flash. I will instantly go into a fear mode. I'll start thinking about death—what is there on the other side, does my consciousness continue after this—and I get terribly, terribly frightened. I feel alone and scared and I don't know what to do. It's very strange; it hits me like a ton of bricks.

Bob: So at that point, do you try to run from it, try to deny it, or what?

Brian: A lot of times I do. I've tried to hide my fear, laughing it off or trying to forget. As long as I can remember I've been terrified by the nuclear threat, the thought that at any moment we could be annihilated. I was so convinced that this one world is all there is, the one science keeps telling us about, and once we get wiped out, that's it—it's total darkness. That scared the socks off me for a long time.

Bob: How did you deal with it?

Brian: I'll be really honest here. I dealt with it in a number of ways. Back in high school and shortly after, I dealt with it with drugs and alcohol—like a lot of people do. I smoked a lot of dope! That took care of it for a while, but eventually you come down off that high and you've got to deal with the real world—you've got to deal with your problems and your pain.

Bob: How about more up to date, in the past year or two: Would it be fair to say a whole new series of insights have come your way?

Brian: Absolutely. When I go into a fear mode, I try to remember all that I have learned and it is sort of a leap of faith. There's a lot of information out there and it's hard to know what's true and what's not. But I reach for my intuition and I go into my own mantra. It's not original, but I remind myself that I am a powerful, immortal spiritual being of love and light. I am a multi-dimensional being. I don't answer to a God or Jesus, or whoever is the doctrine of the day. I answer only to my higher self, and I remind myself that I do have a higher self, that there is more to who I am and that I'm connected to everything. I want to understand more—I want desperately to learn more. I don't always understand what I'm going through. I guess that's why I'm trying to learn, so I can deal with it more productively. When I first took the Flower of Life workshop, almost a year ago, that was a huge, huge step. That changed my life dramatically. I had been to one UFO convention, but that was nothing compared to being with Drunvalo for six days.

A month later I quit my job, and spent time with some Native Americans! It was at the Star Knowledge conference in South Dakota in June 1996. For the first time, I saw all the covert back-stabbing at work and I just couldn't be there anymore. I didn't even give two weeks' notice. They were very kind and let me go. I was so concerned, though, what my friends would think, what my co-workers would think, what my family would think. However, I'm lucky to have some pretty hip friends and family, because at least that core group of people supported me. My dad said he thought it was great that I actually did something spontaneous and had an adventure. He said I needed that. I was so concerned that he would say, "How could you drop everything and be irresponsible?" But he surprised me and I'm grateful for that. He does support me, but he doesn't understand this new learning, this new growth I've been a part of. But he's tolerant. I don't have one family member or friend who really understands what I'm going through or what I think is happening.

Bob: Can you talk about that? You are going through these tremendous changes and your family and friends are not.

Brian: Well, you're exposed to this new learning and you want to share it with the world, but everyone else has their own baggage, their own indoctrinations. I had a conversation with a friend of the family—he's about twenty years older than me and highly educated. We had a theoretical discussion about whether there are ETs, a secret government, etc. He was dealing with theories and possibilities and I was trying to tell him, "Look, I'm beyond that, I know they're here, I've seen and heard enough." I'm trying to get it through people's thick heads, saying don't you see it, can't you hear it, something is happening! And it's really frustrating that people stick to these old doctrines. I don't want to be arrogant about it—that's the last thing I want to do. I believe the process has to be as gentle for everyone as it has been for me. Everyone else is on their own time frame for development. If people want to know, I am more than happy to share. I think I've come to that point. When I have that permission, I will be happy to share as much information as I can. But this past year or two, it has been a real frustrating process.

Bob: Can you talk about some of the interim things you've been through where maybe you didn't have full permission?

Brian: Sure. I finished David Icke's book, . . . *and the truth shall set you free*, and I tried to tell my dad about it. He said, "No, I don't believe it, I think it's all fantasy, all conspiracy

theories." He told me he's concerned about the fact that I
buy into all this stuff. But I don't share that concern when I
intuitively feel that what I'm hearing, reading, and learning
is real, at least for me. It seems a lot more true than the
garbage we get from the media.

Bob: What about when we were hiking on Mount Tamal-
pais. Can you recreate that?

Brian: Yes. That was when we were talking about the
secret government and what's going on with the planet, ETs
and Earth changes and such. You said, "Isn't it just weird to
know all these things, to be a lot more enlightened than you
were a year ago?" It *is* weird to know. I feel like a completely
different person than one or two years ago, a completely different personality. Old friends who haven't seen me for a
while would not know me. They would say, "Get out of here!
You're crazy!"

Bob: Have you found yourself letting go of some old
friendships?

Brian: Yes. I used to have a group of old high school
friends. We were close, we were tight. I miss them dearly, but
we've all gone through changes and we've gone our own
ways. Sometimes the separations were abrupt and painful,
and sometimes we just faded away. And I have new friends
now. I feel closer in a way to my new friends, because we're
on a similar path. That includes friends from UFO conven-
tions, Flower of Life, and I hope that includes a couple of
Native Americans. When I met them in South Dakota last
year and did the sweat lodge, smoked the pipe of friendship,
and did the Sun Dance, that was an amazing experience! The
old friends that I've managed to hold on to—and it's just
barely—tolerate this stuff and then they ask that I move on
to another subject as quickly as possible.

Bob: Can you define "pain" and how you interact with it?

Brian: When I say pain, I mean uncontrollable emotions. They are absolutely uncontrollable and it doesn't last for minutes—it lasts for hours, sometimes days.

Bob: What's your tendency—to run from it, to avoid it and pretend it's not there?

Brian: No, I no longer pretend it's not there.

Bob: But you used to?

Brian: Yes, I used to.

Bob: Can you talk about that? Are you in the process of making a shift in terms of your interaction with "pain"?

Brian: I'd like to think I'm not running. I used to tell myself things like "don't feel that, what's wrong with you, distract yourself." So whatever was happening would take a few minutes before I'd find a way out of it. I'd pat myself on the back for being so clever, but then it would always come back. Lately—and it happens at night a lot—I'm letting a lot of stuff come out.

Bob: You seem to be turning a corner here. Most people would do anything to avoid feeling some things, but you seem to be on the track that's teaching you that it's the opposite that works—going into it and going through it rather than running from it.

Brian: Yes, and some of it is involuntary too. There's also something nudging me, without my consciously knowing about it—something that says, "Get it out, let it go." About eight or nine months ago I started exercising. I had a weight problem and that led to a self-esteem problem. I've had that for a long time, and I finally decided to do something about it. I've been losing weight and I'm real proud of myself. I've noticed that exercising can produce a natural high—and that it can produce a real low, too. Sometimes I wish I had a punching bag in my apartment. . . . Sometimes the littlest things can put me into a complete rage mode. I remember when I was a kid, I liked hitting my dad—it was playful, but I liked punching him. I don't know if it was something he did, or if I just wanted to take out my anger on my father, wherever that anger came from. I hate to admit this, but it seems as though I have a real propensity for violence, and I didn't know I had that in me.

Bob: Is it fair to say that you're going through more changes now and that you're feeling them more intensely in the past year or two, including the violence and anger thing?

Brian: Oh yes. I've had some terrible, terrible thoughts about things I'd want to do to people. At first I'd think, "That's terrible, I shouldn't think that," but then I realized maybe I should just complete it—make friends with it, as you say.

Bob: It is possible that we all have traumatic incompletions from the past that live in the body in the form of what I call "stuck energy." They also live in the mind in the form of thought patterns that become subconscious beliefs about life that unwittingly determine our direction in life. As you become more aware and more conscious, is it possible that some of this old suppressed stuff is being shaken up, so that it's starting to come to the surface for you? Does that seem like a possibility?

Brian: It does seem like a possibility, it really does — especially lately and with more frequency and more intensity. I still can't profess to understand it. Reincarnation is a part of my belief system. I think I've had things happen to me in previous lives, other things that may have even happened to me as an infant in this life. It might have been the birth process itself. I've even suspected alien abduction. There are two scoop marks on my body I can't account for. Getting back to what I'm experiencing and what I think is happening to me—who knows? Was I abused, was I abducted, who was I before I was here, where was I before

I was here? I think about these things all the time. I wish I knew—I don't like being so ignorant.

Bob: Is it fair to say then that emotions have been coming up more powerfully for you than they have in the past?

Brian: I'd say in the past six months I've felt more emotions than I have in the past six years.

Bob: To complete my thoughts on it, as you become more conscious, you can in fact, expect this sort of thing to happen. It's a displacement process. The old stuck energy is being displaced by all the new energy coming in. It's really a simple principle: If you have a glass of water with a layer of mud on the bottom, (old stuck energy) and if you begin pouring in a constant stream of new fresh water (new energy), the first thing that happens is the mud is stirred up and the water becomes muddy. If you continue pouring in the fresh water, eventually all the mud (old stuck energy) will get flushed out and you are left with a glass of fresh pure water (new energy). Does that analogy make sense in terms of the emotional process you're going through? If it does, then would it make sense to find a way to expand your ability to let the process be okay, or even if it's not okay, can you find a way to let it be okay that it's not okay? All of this expands your ability to be with it as it is, which expands your ability to have a thorough experience of it rather than resistance. If you can allow yourself to have a thorough experience, then you are allowing this displacement process to complete itself. You have, in other words, moved through those changes.

Brian: That's a real good analogy; it makes a lot of sense to me. I have a lot of garbage.

Bob: Does it make sense then, given that you are going through this intense and fast-paced process of waking up, that it's stirring up things that used to be on a less-than-conscious level—bringing them up from suppression such that you have all these emotions, as you say, more powerful and more intense

than ever before? Then does it make sense that it's all a function of consciousness, that it's what waking up is supposed to
entail? What it's about then is acknowledging and accepting
the fact that life is full of risk and changes; it's about embrac-
ing it rather than resisting it. So does it make sense to go with
the flow, to go into it rather than resist it?

Brian: Yes, that makes sense. I would agree with that; it
would explain the intense process I'm going through. But
knowing the difference between resistance and moving through
it is something I haven't been able to pinpoint yet. . . . I know
I'm going through something. . . . I don't know if anyone else
is. It feels unique to me, to my own experience.

Bob: That's what everybody says, until I get a group of
people together and ask them. The response is always one
hundred percent. The most recent chance I had to do that
was last Friday night when I gave a talk at East-West Book-
shop. Everyone there rose their hands in unison to the question, "Are you going through intense changes?" Most people
have a tendency to think it's just them.

Brian: That's what I thought: "What's wrong with me?
What's going on with me?" Everyone else seems to manage
okay. They all act like their lives are just peachy-keen. I guess
knowing others are experiencing intense changes makes me
feel better—misery loves company! It's not all pain and sor-
row, but when it comes to that emotion, which is very powerful, sometimes when you get that low, you think you're
never going to come back up out of it. When you do, it's
somewhat of a relief, it feels great. And this new learning
has been a great joy. Spending a week with Drunvalo twice
was awesome! Meeting the other students in the group was
awesome. Even exchanging tapes or watching a new video
is great. And I used to resist learning. Maybe beneath the
surface I knew it was all a steaming pile of dog flop. Maybe
I couldn't stand what I was learning. But then, a couple of

years ago, I met some enlightened people; I started opening up and I took a look at a few new things. From then on, my passion for learning has grown and grown. It's like a new person was born. As a result, it makes sense that I would go through the emotional changes too. This has been a wonderful adventure, even with all its highs and lows. I wouldn't change it for anything, I wouldn't go back, I can't go back. I don't know about you—would you want to forget what you've learned? Would you say, "Please erase my memory for the past ten to fifteen years?" No. Like you said on the phone, you've had fifteen to twenty years to learn how to go through all this. You said to me, "Brian, you've only had about two years to go through this."

Listen to those crickets! You know, a lot of times when someone approaches these guys, they shut up. But we're just sitting here yapping away and they're singing! Very cool!

Bob: I want to thank them; I've enjoyed it.

Brian: Me too! Maybe they're going through their emotional-body clearing and they're completely turned around, singing when the sun is still up, when they normally sing at night. Listen to them, they're all over us! I think that means something.

Thank you, Brian, for a great time, for a great interview, and for making the points more clearly than I could.

If any of you find yourselves going through any of the changes Brian is; if you find yourself feeling more and stronger emotions with greater mood swings, if you find some old friendships falling away, if you don't always know how to deal with friends and family, if you are thinking it's just you, and if you are wondering what's wrong with you—relax! It's happening to all of us!

Again, this is a time of tremendous change, for the planet, and for its people, individually and collectively. No one can escape it; no amount of denial, avoidance, hiding, or resistance will ultimately work. The key then, as always, is consciousness.

The first step to consciousness is awareness. If you don't know or understand the process, then you will forever be at the effect of it. You will avoid, resist, deny, go into fear, wonder what's wrong with you, or wonder what others will think, etc.

If you do understand, then you can learn to interact with the process consciously. You can learn how to benefit fully from whatever is going on by learning how to go with it and ultimately through it. That is called emotional-body clearing, and that is what most of the rest of this book is about.

Here is Drunvalo speaking at the Star Visions Conference in Estes Park, Colorado, in November of 1996:

> In the work that we do through the Flower of Life . . .
> [The Flower of Life] program was designed to integrate
> the left and right brain and to show the mind how all
> things are interconnected, so that they could see the
> unity. But the area that we did not expand upon was the
> area of the emotional body—this is our biggest prob-
> lem. Our biggest challenge right now is to find balance
> through these changes. We talk about using the mer-
> kaba—but even that is not enough if the emotional body
> is unbalanced. We could know the merkaba perfectly,
> but if you can't keep your emotional balance it's not
> going to help a lot.

Also from Drunvalo, in response to a question about the photon belt:

> We are not going to enter into any external field of light
> and be transformed in such a way that we escape our
> karmic bonds. We are going to have to work with our

emotions and all the various things that we have done —down here on Earth, right in the mud and the murk— and get through this stuff before we are able to enter into these higher levels of existence.

The foundation of our discussion has been set. We are now able to proceed to the main theme, which is emotional-body clearing.

We all have incompletions from the past that continue to shape our lives until they are unraveled. I will first spell out the sources of these incompletions and how they affect us; then we will look at ways of moving through or healing these consciousness inhibitors.

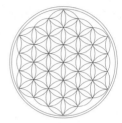

9

THE MIND

Don't change beliefs. Transform the believer.
— Werner Erhard

This is the beginning of the second half of the book—and it really is like a second book.

I spent a lot of time wondering how to do this. There are many good books on emotional-body clearing, so how could I offer a unique contribution? It took me back to the summer of 1989 when I didn't think I could do much more than rehash what had already been said.

Then I realized that the only way I can write a book on emotional-body clearing is just the way I'm doing: using the first half to properly set the stage—that is, life is not as it appears, there's more going on than just finding the right relationship, or the right job, or the right car, etc. . . . My point is that we need to see emotional-body clearing in the context of the bigger picture.

But I was still wondering how to do the second half. For me, writing a book is a continual matter of trusting and letting go, or in other words, giving up control. It has always been my experience that doing so leads to true control. It's about going with the skid, instead of slamming on your brakes and forcing the issue.

So I keep remembering just to tell it like it happened in my life. There's no need to try and be too clever here.

To really tell it I have to go back to the early 1970s, a time when one of my main interests in life was bowling. I was very serious about my bowling game. I even tried the professional tour for a while in 1970–71. After six tournaments, I came away with a low back injury and the realization that most pros were better than I was.

I realized that my mind was my greatest enemy. My body knew, my muscles knew—my natural knowingness knew how to make the shot—but often my mind wouldn't let me, especially, of course, in pressure situations. So I felt that my greatest need was to learn to quiet my mind and just be there with my natural ability.

My first breakthrough came from a friend who was aware of my plight. He said that if I was really interested in learning about the mind I should check out Alan Watts. He recommended I read one book in particular called simply, *The Book*.[1] So I ran off to a local bookstore; in fact, I looked in two or three bookstores, but I couldn't find *The Book*. I wasn't really sure there was such a title anyway—who would ever name a book *The Book*? So I came home with a book by Watts called *This Is It*.[2] I figured I must have the right one. But my friend said, "No, this isn't it; it's *The Book*!"

So I tried a bookstore on the other side of town and found it. Then I went home and started reading. I couldn't put it down. It was absolutely what I was looking for. It became my bible, my constant companion for at least the next year.

The full title of the book is *The Book: On the Taboo Against Knowing Who You Are*. To quote from the back cover:

> Perhaps the most famous of all Watts' works, *The Book* delves into the cause and cure of the illusion that the self is a separate ego, housed in a bag of skin, which "confronts" a universe of physical objects which are alien and stupid. According to Dr. Watts, this illusion underlies the misuse of technology for a violent and hostile subjugation of man's natural environment, leading to its eventual destruction. . . .With his customary lucidity and wit, Alan Watts presents the "lowdown" on the nature of the self in the form of *The Book*—a manual of initiation into the central mystery of existence which any father might slip to his son, or mother to her daughter, upon the threshold of adult life.[3]

And that's really how it all began. That was the beginning of a journey that continues to this day. And all I wanted was to be a better bowler!

Actually, I did have an idea prior to my discovery of Watts, and that was to quiet the mind by learning to go into an alpha state. I didn't know how to do that, but a bowling friend, my "mind coach," gave me a book on transcendental meditation. In 1974 I took the TM course and about two seconds into my first meditation I realized I had discovered something really powerful. My bowling instantly improved, dramatically so.

This all happened between 1972 and 1974, and if you are familiar with the 1972 chapter in *Nothing*, you will recall that this was a time of tremendous change on the planet.

During that period, the Sirians intended for us to evolve as quickly as possible. In fact, for a brief time they even took away our free will. We were like little children playing with guns, and for a while they said, "No, you can't do that." Then they began to program events into our lives that would enable us to evolve as quickly as possible. Shortly thereafter, they gave us back our free will, sort of. What they did in fact was to provide us a menu of options, and if we picked the wrong one, they would keep offering us the same choices until we picked the right one.

What I know for sure is that 1972 through 1974 was a time of tremendous change and growth for me. It didn't feel as though I was being forced to do anything, either. The motivation was coming from me. Remember, I was mainly an aspiring bowler.

Then I heard about *est* (Erhard Seminars Training). Actually, it was difficult not to hear about *est;* in 1975 it was big. It seemed to just come out of nowhere—all of a sudden, there was this thing called *est*. Everyone seemed to have an opinion of it too. People were either pro or con; no one was neutral.

My own initial opinion was negative. *est* seemed to me like fast food. I thought that in order to get enlightened you probably had to study with a Zen master and then spend twenty years or so sitting on a hilltop or in a cave. How could two weekends possibly transform your life? No way! I had also heard that the *est* introductory seminars were more than a little like attending an Amway rally—that really turned me off.

Then a close friend—in fact, the same friend who turned me on to Alan Watts—took the training. Of course, I was eager to hear his opinion. He told me in a way that I could trust and understand that there really was something to *est,* and that maybe I should check it out.

So I did. I went to an introductory seminar. My friend and I had talked enough previously to convince me that I was going to enroll. It's a good thing we did. It was worse than an Amway rally! And I'm sure they gave toasters to the people who brought the most guests! Furthermore, they were pushy! They would have said they were only giving me an opportunity to choose, but I say they were pushy!

Even though I knew I was going to enroll, I was determined not to succumb in those circumstances. So I waited until the next morning. I went down to the *est* office and handed in my enrollment papers, along with a check. I was in the training.

My friend had prepared me, as best he could, on what to expect. Essentially what he said was, "Don't be fooled by the props; it's not as it appears; there is something else going on."

I learned from our discussions not to be fooled by the trainer and assistants. He said they will do anything they can to unsettle you, and not to be taken in by that. He recommended that if I looked upon them as actors playing roles, at the very least I would be thoroughly entertained. I did and I was.

The *est* training was held on consecutive Saturdays and Sundays, beginning promptly at 8:30 AM and running often until the early hours of the morning. Each day lasted however long it took for the particular day's information to be transmitted. There was also a three-hour pre-training meeting, a Wednesday evening mid-training meeting, and a post-training meeting.

My training was held in a ballroom on the second floor of the student union on the campus of the University of California at Berkeley. There were approximately two hundred and fifty people present.

On day one, promptly at 8:30 AM a zombie-like character marched up to the stage. I'm guessing about the time, as one of our agreements was no timepieces in the training room, but since *est* is *always* on time, I was quite certain that our training began promptly.

"MY NAME IS VICTOR. I AM HERE TO ASSIST YOUR TRAINER. YOUR TRAINING HAS NOW BEGUN."

Even though Victor was neatly dressed, he looked as though he had just crawled out of a casket. He looked like and, better yet, acted like a zombie. He spent at least an hour reminding us, in a totally monotone and mechanical voice, of each of our previously consented-upon agreements. At a pre-training seminar we had gone over and consented to these agreements, so we already knew them.

The gist of the agreements was that we would remain in the room until the training was over for the day; we would not talk unless we were sharing in the agreed-upon way; there would be no bathroom breaks until the trainer said so; and we would only eat at the meal break, of which there would be a maximum of one and a minimum of none. People went nuts over these last two agreements. It reminded me of what Alan Watts said in *The Book:*

> There is a growing apprehension that existence is a rat-race in a trap: living organisms, including people, are merely tubes which put things in at one end and let them out at the other, which both keeps them doing it and in the long run wears them out. So to keep the farce going, the tubes find ways of making new tubes, which also put things in at one end and let them out at the other. At the input end they even develop ganglia of nerves called brains, with eyes and ears, so that they can more easily scrounge around for things to swallow. As and when they get enough to eat, they use up their surplus energy by wiggling in complicated patterns, making all sorts of noises by blowing air in and out of the input hole, and gathering together in groups to fight with other groups. In time, the tubes grow such an abundance of attached appliances that they are hardly recognizable as mere tubes, and they manage to do this in a staggering variety of forms. There is a vague rule not to eat tubes of your own form, but in general there is serious competition as to who is going to be the top type of tube. All

this seems marvelously futile, and yet, when you begin to think about it, it begins to be more marvelous than futile. Indeed, it seems extremely odd.[4]

Maybe there's more to life than merely satisfying our "tubeness." *est* certainly thought so.

Then in the middle of Victor's monologue, a very neatly dressed man in his mid-thirties came marching up from the back of the room. "THAT'S WHY YOUR LIVES DON'T WORK! IT'S LIKE YOU PAID $300 FOR A NEW RADIO; VICTOR IS TRYING TO TELL YOU HOW THE RADIO WORKS, AND YOU ASSHOLES AREN'T EVEN LISTENING! YOU THINK YOUR WAY IS BETTER! MY NAME IS RON. I AM YOUR TRAINER!"

By this time, almost everyone was squirming and turning in their seat. Some people looked as though they were ready to leave. I'm sitting there thinking, "Boy, this is great! It's even better than I thought it would be!"

Ron turned out to be absolutely the most imposing, the most impressive person I had ever met. This all happened in November 1977. I remember much of it as though it happened last week.

Notes

1. Alan Watts, *The Book: On the Taboo Against Knowing Who You Are* (New York: Random House, 1966).

2. Alan Watts, *This Is It* (New York: Random House, 1958).

3. Watts, *The Book*. Back cover.

4. Ibid., p. 5.

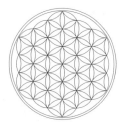

10

GETTING IT

> *It's much easier to ride the horse in the*
> *direction he's going.* — Werner Erhard

So what did I get from *est*? Well, first I "got" that there are lots of trappings in *est*, lots of pitfalls to "getting it," including the jargon. If you have taken *est*, you know what I mean.

One of the criticisms of *est*, and there were many, was that it created a bunch of junior trainers who thought their job in life was to go around handling other people's cases in mock trainer fashion—everyone's case but their own, that is. My friends and I later turned that into a joke: "See, that's why your life doesn't work—that's why you're an asshole!" That line was usually good for a laugh. It was usually delivered with reverence too; I think it reminded us of the great experience the training was. I don't recall ever meeting an *est* graduate who didn't admire and respect their trainer.

But the true value of *est* lay beneath the joking and the gesturing, of course. It was a priceless opportunity to experience directly the "acts" that we all are, in a setting of safety and trust so that we could let go of them.

By the way, let me be clear that I was there on an "act" too. Being above it all and "unaffected" by the trainer was my act, a sort of armoring that served as a buffer. It kept me in my head, in my concepts of life, and protected me from having to experience my emotions.

Nonetheless, I did get a great deal of value from the training. Much of what I know about the mind and routinely teach today in the Flower of Life workshop and in rebirthing came from *est*. Additionally, almost everyone in the early days of rebirthing was an *est* graduate and deeply influenced by it. It therefore had a major impact on rebirthing. I will spell that out as we go along.

Leonard Orr was even an *est* staff member for a brief period in 1975. Somehow he and Werner Erhard met. Werner was impressed enough to hire Leonard as a special consultant to the trainers.

est was not about being reasonable. In fact, our "reasonableness" was confronted every step of the way, beginning with the agreements. In addition to the previously mentioned agreements, we were asked not to sit next to anyone we knew. We agreed not to take notes or tape any of the training; to remain in our chairs at all times unless otherwise instructed; and not to use alcohol or any drugs other than prescribed medication for the duration of the training. When asked the purpose of these agreements—and people did ask—Victor would only answer, "Because that's what works."

What most of us heard in these agreements were rules handed down by an authority figure (parent, teacher, etc.), because most people are at the effect of something I will discuss later called the parental disapproval syndrome (Chapter 11), either rebelling against or conforming to authority figures.

We were asked to take responsibility for the agreements—to treat them as though they were our own, as though we had determined for ourselves that they were the conditions necessary to create a foundation that would allow us to get maximum value from the training.

However, most of us were used to agreements that were reasonable. For example, most people would consider it reasonable to have a watch in your coat or in your handbag at the back of the room. Minimally, ten to twenty people acknowledged at some point that they had broken the agreement about not having a watch in the room.

We were given many opportunities to see that reasonableness is at the bottom of the barrel of non-experienced experience—that it is living life conceptually, it is being at effect, it is being in survival, it is giving our power away. Reasonableness is victim consciousness. "I didn't do it because I couldn't do it, or because there was too much traffic and I was late," or—whatever. We act as though our reasons for not doing it are what matters. We fail to see that what matters is whether or not we did it.

Another factor in all this agreement stuff is what Werner calls the "ruthless rules of reality." Werner says these rules are not reasonable; they just are. Gravity, for example, doesn't care if you fall off a ladder and break your leg. It may be unfair or unreasonable, but much of life is constructed in that manner. It doesn't work to blame gravity.

Victor was just standing up front being the ruthless rules of reality, and people were going nuts! Victor didn't care.

So as Ron would say, "Your lives don't work because you are living mechanically in your belief systems rather than in your experiences."

He then went on to tell a famous *est* story: If you put a rat in a maze with cheese at the end of the fourth tunnel, after a while the rat will learn to find the cheese. Humans can learn that too. If the cheese is moved to a different tunnel, the rat will continue to look down the fourth tunnel until the rat eventually learns to look elsewhere. The difference between rats and humans is that humans will continue to look down the fourth tunnel forever because humans have developed a belief in the fourth tunnel. Rats, on the other hand, don't believe in anything—all they want is cheese.

So we live our lives out of concepts and beliefs and not from experience. And the lowest form of non-experience is reasonableness. Ron diagrammed all this on a blackboard as follows (Fig. 10-1): First he drew a horizontal line and labeled it "nothing." Just below the line was the label "non-experience." Then he wrote "helping, hoping, deciding," and "reasonableness" in descending order. These he called the different levels of non-experience.

Just above the horizontal line he wrote "accepting." As described in *The Book of est:*

> Above the line is an *experienced* experience, and the first step above the line, the first form of experience, involves simply accepting. If you want to get out of the realm of non-experienced experience, you've got to stop being reasonable, stop making decisions, stop hoping, and just *accept what is.* No more, no less. Accept what is. When you do that, the light bulb of experience is turned on. Until you do, it's turned off.[1]

Above "accepting," Ron wrote "witnessing or observing." Above that he wrote "participation or sharing," and at the top was "sourcing." These are the different levels of experienced experiences.

The Book of est says that if you use a scale of one to one hundred to measure experience and non-experience, "reasonableness" would be minus eighty. "Deciding" would be minus twenty, "hoping" minus ten, and "helping" minus five on the scale. "Accepting" would be plus five on the side of experience, all the way up to one hundred for "sourcing."

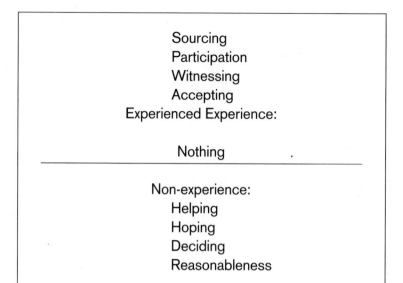

Figure 10-1. The different levels of experience.

In order to get from minus to plus, you have to go through zero or nothing. To get from non-experience to experience then, you have to go through nothing, the great void!

> The purpose of the *est* training is to transform your ability to experience living, so that the situations you have been trying to change or have been putting up with clear up just in the process of life itself.[2]

I remember how Ron spent plenty of time explaining what he meant by the words "transform" and "change," and then getting examples from various trainees of situations they had been putting up with or trying to change. A great ray of hope spread across the room as people considered the possibility that persistently difficult situations could actually clear up. Of course, if anyone expressed hopefulness, Ron would quickly point out that hope is in the realm of non-experience.

The Book of est states that:

> ... the word transform doesn't mean "change," it means
> —"transubstantiate" or "alter the substance of your
> ability to experience living." Change implies only mod-
> ification of form. We're talking about something as rad-
> ical as the difference between plus one and minus one.
> Going from minus five to minus one—we can call that
> change. But going from minus one to plus one—that
> represents a one-hundred-and-eighty-degree turnabout.
> That represents a transformation of your ability to expe-
> rience living. And to get from minus one to plus one
> you've got to go through nothing.[3]

Later in the day, we did our first process. Ron instructed
us to locate a space in the toe of our left foot. After a few seconds, he said, "Good," and then instructed us to locate a space
in the bone of our left foot, and so on, throughout our bodies.

It seemed simple enough, yet it was impossible not to
notice that some people were sniffing and crying. "Why are
people becoming emotional?" I wondered. My answer came
less than two years later when I discovered through rebirthing
that we all have incompletions from the past which live in
the body in the form of stuck energy. As this "stuckness"
builds, people increasingly withdraw awareness from their
bodies. This means that most of us are not in our bodies. This
process in *est* gave people an opportunity to experience their
bodies, and for some, it had been a long time. Of course, I
had no clue myself at the time—I wasn't in my body, either.

Then came the three notions of *est*. According to *The Book
of est* the first notion is: "You are perfect—but there are barriers preventing you from experiencing and expressing your
perfection." The second notion is: "Resistance leads to persistence. If you try to resist something or change something,
it will become more solid. The only way to get rid of some-

thing is just to let it be. This doesn't mean to ignore it. Ignoring is actually a form of rejection and resistance . . . . To let something be means to observe it, stay in touch with it, but make no effort to change it." The third notion is: "The re-creation of an experience makes the experience disappear. Re-experiencing something to completion disappears it."4

Regarding the second notion, there are various forms of resistance. They include avoidance, denial, trying to change, trying to get rid of, trying to control, using will power, being a positive thinker, learning to live with it, trying to solve it, ignoring it, distracting yourself, suppressing it, and trying to cover it up with other behavior.

So if you have a persistent problem such as anger, fear, or any other unwanted emotion, tension, headaches, bodily sensations, illness, unwanted thoughts, unwanted behavior, etc., and if you resist it in any way, you will lock the energy in place and become stuck with it for as long as you resist it.

Now that's very interesting, given that we are in the midst of polarity consciousness. We have been taught to resist or judge EVERYTHING!

With respect to the third notion, if you can allow yourself to have a thorough experience of your persistent, recurring problem, it will disappear. In order to do this, you need to re-create it—that is, totally experience it, element by element. You observe it, witness it, and be with it, letting it be the way it is without trying to change it. You get in touch with your bodily sensations—what they feel like and exactly where they are in your body. Additionally, you get in touch with the size, shape, weight, and color of these sensations. You do the same thing with emotions. Emotions feel like something in your body.

Remembering this fact is critical. All bodily sensations, emotions, etc.—let's call them symptoms—are a healing in process. Such symptoms are old stuck energy from the past coming up out of suppression (into activation) for healing. You get the healing (disappearance) by going into them and experiencing (feeling) them fully.

This is incredibly important given that we have been taught the opposite. If you fully understand this, prescription drugs and doctors become optional at best. This understanding is really the bottom line in rebirthing; it is what allows the process to work. I will explain in Chapter 12.

At one point near the end of the first day, Ron brought a volunteer with a headache to the front of the room. This person sat in a chair next to Ron. Ron had him get in touch with his headache by locating it exactly in his body. He then asked, "What size is it, what shape, what color, how much water will it hold?" over and over until the headache disappeared.

Day two was mainly about processes. The first was the "truth process," in which we were all given an opportunity to disappear a persistent, recurring problem. Many people discovered that when their problem disappeared, underneath it was a more basic problem—an incompletion from the past. Since their problem was not in present time, the process of eradicating it was like peeling the layers of an onion.

Next came the "danger process," in which groups of twenty-five or so people took turns standing in the front of the room, just "being" with the rest of the trainees. This was a tremendous confrontation for most of the trainees, myself included. Then for toppers, eight zombie-like assistants came up to the front of the room. Each picked a trainee and stood nose-to-nose with them in order to "be" with them. Of course, Ron was constantly yelling at us to get off our acts and just be with them. People went crazy! I was one of the fortunate ones who got to "be" with a zombie. I remember trying to turn the tables on my zombie by just staring into his eyes. It didn't work—he stood there, no emotions, no expressions, just a perfect upright corpse.

Then came the "fear process." We lay on the floor with our eyes closed and were instructed to fill ourselves with fear (real or imagined)—to in fact be terrified of the people lying next to us. We were instructed to act this fear out, and to keep extending it until we were petrified of everyone in the entire room, then everyone in the city, the state, the country, the entire planet!

Next Ron reversed it, telling us that the people lying next to us were afraid of us; then that everyone in the room, and of course everyone on the planet, was deathly afraid of each one of us. And he really played it up, until it became a huge joke. We had created so much fear that we were able to "be" with it and laugh at it.

That was it for the evening, or should I say morning. It was 3:30 AM. That is, except for Victor. We had seen nothing of him since the last bathroom break, when he mechanically reminded us of our "bathroom break agreements."

So it's 3:30 AM (approximately—we got out at 4 AM, so I'm guessing) and it's time to "handle rides." Everybody's favorite zombie, Victor, is in charge of "handling rides." He did it with all the charm and charisma you would expect from the Ruthless Rules of Reality. Then we were out of there!

I left the training that night on an incredible high, and it seemed that everyone else did too. I could hardly wait for the next weekend!

At 8:30 AM on the second Saturday, there was Victor, doing his "gravity" act again. But wait a minute—the person who followed him to the stage was not Ron.

"MY NAME IS HAL. I AM NOT RON! I AM YOUR TRAINER THIS WEEKEND!"

Ron had definitely made it to the top of my list of superheroes. During the five "off" days I found myself constantly wondering, "What would Ron think, or how would Ron handle this situation?" And now Ron wasn't even here and we got this guy Hal instead? Hal didn't measure up. Why, he even had to use a portable microphone. Ron didn't have to; he could project his voice whether he screamed or whispered. Hal couldn't. And so it was. I spent a lot of time noticing that Hal wasn't Ron.

Evidently this switching of trainers was done on a regular basis. It was done in each of the mock trainings I took later.

I recall in my first mock training, about midway through the third day, we decided our new trainer just wasn't being tough enough with us. Ron *never* would have put up with the guff we were giving this guy. Why, even Hal would have called us assholes by now! So we decided it was time to "train" him. We created a situation in which he had no choice but to yell at us. When he finally barked out, " ... and that's why you're assholes!" we spontaneously rose in a standing ovation. From that point on, the training was a joyous celebration.

Much of the third day was about reality. After a lengthy discussion on the nature of reality, we came to a three-fold test for reality. *The Book of est* describes this test as follows:

> First, it's *physical*. We don't call something real unless it's physical. Physicalness manifests itself in time, distance, and form. Things that are physical have form, they exist in time, and they cover or occupy a distance. ....
> Secondly, the substance of physicalness is *measurability*. That is to say, time, form, and distance all necessitate the ability to measure, and when something is measurable it simply means it has a beginning, a middle, and an end.
> ... Thirdly, the substance of measurability is *agreement*. For something to be measurable it must have a beginning. And all beginnings follow an end which is preceded by a middle.
>
> ... This blackboard is *real* because of its physicalness. ... it has form, it exists in time, it has location,

distance, and it is measurable: it has a beginning, middle, and end.⁵

After more discussion on the nature of reality, Hal brought five trainees to the stage and lined them up, all facing the same direction, with the first four tightly packed, and the fifth trainee about two feet behind them. He shoved the first person, creating a falling domino effect—the first four all toppled backwards into the arms of the fifth person.

Then Hal asked, "From the point of view of the fourth person, why did he fall into the arms of the fifth person?"

"Because the third person fell into him," said a trainee.

"Yes, the third person *causes* the *effect* of the fourth person falling into the fifth person. He experiences himself as the effect of number three. What about number three? How does he view this?"

"Number two did it." And so the argument went, all the way to number one, who *caused* the *effect* of number two falling, which is the *cause* of the *effect* of number three falling, which is the *cause* of the *effect* of number four falling.

Of course, it was Hal who *really* did it, but then he was only operating off Werner's instructions and so on. You could probably take this back to the beginning of time. What you really have here is a situation where there is no cause. It's all effect, effect, effect, effect, etc.

> In this type of analysis it's all effect. There never is a cause. And this is the type of analysis you've been using all your lives. It's the one that goes with our reality....We call it "FALSE CAUSE," and it's what you've been letting run your lives.⁶

The discussion turned to the nature of unreality. It seemed reasonable to conclude that unreality must be the opposite of reality. Unreality therefore must not be physical, not measurable, and not dependent on agreement. Furthermore, if reality is effect, effect, effect, etc. —unreality must be cause, cause, cause, etc.

"What is unreality?" we were asked.

"Experience," said a trainee.

"Yes, experience," repeated Hal. "Unreality is experience; it's not physical, it's not measurable, and it's not dependent on agreement."

This had all been written down on a blackboard—on one side, all the characteristics of reality, and on the other side, the characteristics of unreality, which, we agreed, was experience.

Then Hal said, "Is anything wrong here?"

He went to the board, and in best *est* fashion, crossed out the word REALITY and put over it the word UNREAL-ITY. Then he drew a line through UNREALITY and put over it the word REALITY.

Why? Because, as he went on to say, "Experience is the most real thing there is; it's the source of everything. And what most people call reality is based solely upon agreement. If enough people agree that the world is flat, then it's flat."

He then told us not to let this little secret out of the room, that whenever we talk about the unreal physical universe, we should call it by its code word—"reality." And when we speak of our experiences, we use that code word—"unreality."

The next question was, "Who is the source or cause of your experience?"

Of course, the answer is us—each one of us creates our own experience.

This led to a lengthy discussion—it was as if people were looking for loopholes, situations they couldn't possibly have created.

Whether it is completely understood or not, being the sole creator of our experience is something we all have to come to terms with. It begins with the idea of responsibility. I don't see responsibility as a burden; I see it always and only as an opportunity. There is, for example, responsibility that goes with being a licensed driver—you have to follow the rules of the road and be responsible for the consequences. But that responsibility provides an opportunity. It opens up a whole new world of possibilities.

Even if you can logically prove situations in which you did not create the reality, when someone else *really* did it to you and you've been blaming them for it ever since—you are just fooling yourself. Blame = resistance = lock the energy in place = stuck with it = give your power away = victim consciousness.

If you want to step up to source, you must take responsibility for what you have created. In so doing, you claim it and you are it! Your word becomes law in your universe.

We do create our reality unerringly, and taking responsibility for it opens up a whole possibility—it enables us to complete the past instead of being at the effect of it. That, in turn, enables us to be in the present. At that point you will find yourself riding the horse in the direction he's going.

The remainder of the third day was filled with processes, two or three of them. The one I remember best was the one during which groups of twenty or so took turns standing in the front of the room in a straight line, making complete fools of ourselves. We were given a scenario and then instructed to act it out. Hal presented the script—we were to repeat it exactly—and *dramatically*.

My group was given a situation in which we had gotten up in the morning, probably with a terrible hangover, and gone into the bathroom to find a totally unacceptable situation. We were to scream: "DON'T YOU EVER, EVER, EVER, LET ME CATCH YOU BRUSHING YOUR DOG'S TEETH WITH MY TOOTHBRUSH AGAIN!!!"

I screamed and gestured and practically did cartwheels with every word. I was hoarse for the rest of the day, but I did pass the audition.

Those who did not pass got to do it solo, until they got it right. Hal was a stern judge. (By now I noticed that Hal was getting much better; he still wasn't Ron, but he was improving.) For those unfortunate few singled out for repeat performances, this was even more confrontative than the "danger process."

The day ended when Mr. Personality, Victor, mechanically "handled" our rides.

Day four, the final day, was about the anatomy of the mind—eighty-five percent of the training, according to Hal. In fact, he told us to forget the first three days, because this was really it!

The question was, "What is the mind?" Of course *est* had a ready-made answer. "The mind is a linear arrangement of multisensory total records of successive moments of now."[7]

Essentially what this means is that the mind is a stack of tapes: complete records of past experiences that include all the senses. For some of these events we have conscious recall; for others, we don't.

According to *The Book of est*, the purpose, or more accurately, the design function of the mind is survival: "the survival of the being, or of anything which the being considers itself to be."[8]

If the being comes to identify itself with the mind, you have ego, and at that point, the purpose of the mind becomes its own survival.

> Because now the purpose of the mind becomes the survival of the mind itself, the survival of the records, the *tapes*, of the *points of view* of the mind, of the *decisions* of the mind, of the *thoughts*, of the conclusions and

beliefs of the mind. Now the mind has a vested interest in all these. What it does to try to survive is to try to keep itself intact, replay the same tapes, prove itself right. That becomes now the purpose of the mind: to survive by again and again proving itself right.[9]

Additionally, "the mind wants agreement in order to survive. It wants reconfirmation of its point of view, of its *decisions*, of its *conclusions*. It wants to keep proving itself right."[10]

The next question concerned the construction of the mind. It was decided that there are actually two stacks of tapes—one necessary for survival, and the other not necessary for survival. Given that the design function of the mind is its own survival, it would consider the first stack to be more important than the second, because the mind will play the survival tape whenever it feels threatened.

In the necessary-for-survival stack, there are three different possibilities. They are labeled by *est* as a number one, number two, or a number three experience.

A number one experience is the most basic threat to survival, involving pain, impact, and relative unconsciousness. Relative unconsciousness means "anything from full unconsciousness as in sleep to the sort of semiconsciousness we experience when under extreme pain or when under a partial anesthesia."[11]

Examples from childhood could include any type of accident—falling out of a tree, a bicycle or auto accident, getting beat up, etc. But as we have known for years in rebirthing, the earliest and most significant number one incident is birth! I will detail that completely in the next chapter.

A number two experience "is one in which the mind experiences a sudden shocking loss accompanied by strong emotion, usually negative. The easiest examples are the sudden

deaths—to a child all deaths are sudden and unexpected—
of a father or mother or brother."[12]

A number three is any experience that reminds the mind
of an earlier number one. Since a number three is associated
with a number one experience, examples from birth would
include anything reminiscent of the trauma of your birth:
hospitals, doctors, nurses, surgical gloves, forceps, the color
of the walls in the delivery room, getting spanked, etc. That
means, for example, that upsets are never for the reason you
think they are, because they are never in present time. Any
upset is a past number one experience getting triggered. At
that point it is a threat to survival associated with pain, impact,
and relative unconsciousness, which results in the mind
mechanically playing an old survival tape. From an earlier
number one incident we formed certain conclusions about
how we need to behave in case that situation ever presents
itself again. The tape contains a complete record of how we
survived. Since it worked once, the mind reasons it will work
again. It is operating solely on a stimulus-response basis.

Then Hal was interested in discussing the relative sizes
of the two stacks of tapes. How many records are there in
the necessary-for-survival stack, and how many in the stack
not necessary for survival?

He proceeded with a very logical argument, beginning at
birth with an imaginary person. It was acknowledged that
there would be records of this person's birth, which would
be stored in the stack necessary for survival, and that there
would probably be some reminders of his birth (number
threes), along with maybe another number one incident. But
it was also assumed that this infant would have plenty of
records of experiences not necessary for survival—situations
where he was playing and having a good time, where nothing came up to remind him of his birth. They, of course, would
be in the other stack.

Hal asked us to consider the percentage of records that would be contained in the first stack, as compared to the records unnecessary for survival.

Various estimates were tossed around by the trainees. Hal decided on the lowest figure of five percent—not that it was true; it was simply the lowest reasonable figure that anyone gave, and Hal was being very reasonable. So we agreed then that after one year, five percent of this infant's experiences were recorded in the necessary-for-survival stack.

The next question involved considering what would happen in the next three years of this young person's life. It was agreed for the sake of argument that this youngster had a pretty easy life and had only one additional number one experience in these years.

So by age four, our child has had three number ones, and a few number twos—both of which could trigger several number three incidents, given that a number three can be anything the mind associates with a one or a two.

We then considered the percentage of his experiences between ages one and four that would be ones, twos, or threes. The lowest figure given was twenty-five percent, and it became the agreed-upon percentage.

We agreed that for the next three years of this child's life the percentage of ones, twos, and threes can only increase. "If after birth there are, for example, one hundred different stimuli that can trigger ones, twos, or threes, and at the end of one year there are, say, a thousand, and after four years, forty thousand, the number of experiences that can escape being number ones, twos, or threes keeps getting smaller and smaller, and the percentage of experiences which are number ones, twos, or threes gets larger and larger."[13] This means the percentages will continue to grow at least at the rate they have, which means that by age seven, at the latest, all of our young person's experiences will be in the stack necessary for survival.

But at this point, Hal "remembers" that he has forgotten something, the illogical logic of the mind.

> . . . after the royal number one experience of birth, the child has at least a hundred stimuli which would trigger a one, two, or three experience. But with the mind's logic of identity each of these stimuli is immediately associated in the baby's mind with everything else it is related to. The doctor's hands get associated with men's hands, get associated with men's arms, get associated with men, get associated with human beings, and so on and on. The green of the hospital wall gets associated with green leaves, with trees, then with bushes, and so on. The hospital walls get associated with all walls, with all surfaces, and so on. If we honestly look at what happens from the moment of birth onwards we'll see that *everything* the baby experiences from then on is associated with pain, threat to survival, and relative unconsciousness, that everything the baby experiences from birth on is at least a number three experience and thus *all* of the baby's records are in the stack "necessary for survival" and thus all of his behavior is of the mechanical stimulus-response variety.[14]

That means that we are totally mechanical in our nature. Like Pavlov's dogs, we operate solely on a stimulus-response basis. When we hear the "gong," we "salivate." We are machines—it's all we've ever been and it's all we'll ever be.

Hal, by the way, did not miss the opportunity—he played this one to the hilt. He was definitely getting better by now. He still wasn't Ron, though.

These incompletions from the past (ones, twos, and threes) and the conclusions we have formed about life from them become the lens through which we see life. It's as though we put on a pair of dark glasses and then forgot that we did it—

everything in life will look dark—everything we see is shaped, molded, and formed by the lens we are unknowingly wearing, and we think that it's just the way life is.

For us, life is seen through the lens called the trauma of birth. It becomes a context for our lives which was created unknowingly and unconsciously. The content in our lives then is unwittingly shaped and formed by that context.

The difference between an enlightened person and an unenlightened person is that the enlightened one knows he or she is a machine, while the unenlightened person is trying to prove he isn't. Once you discern the mechanical nature of the mind, you can choose not to identify with it, or at least choose not to take it quite so seriously.

If you *choose* your mechanical nature, then you are no longer at the effect of it and no longer resisting it. Remember, resistance equals persistence. Choosing your situation, on the other hand, enables you to *be* with it. That in turn allows you to have a thorough experience of it, which leads to completion or the disappearance of the situation. What will begin to happen is that situations you have been putting up with, or have been trying to change, will clear up just in the process of life itself. That in turn will start the process of chipping away at more deeply rooted number ones. You are unraveling the ball of yarn, rather than adding to it.

As you unravel the ball, what you are left with is space—space to be and space from which to create. All this space to create comes from nothing. All along Ron and Hal told us we would get nothing from the training, and they were right, of course.

Until you get "nothing" there is no space to create. You are below the line and in the realm of unexperienced experience. What you have there is something, and you cannot create from something. You can only create from nothing.

So you are a machine! Get it?

Regarding choice, most of us have no idea what it is. We think choice is that we like this one better, or because we tried that one yesterday, we will try this one today. That is nothing more than our reasons or our considerations deciding for us, which puts us squarely into the realm of false cause. At that point we are coming from our mechanical survival tapes of effect—effect—effect—etc.

Stepping out of being at the effect of life opens up the possibility of experiencing yourself as the source, the one who is unerringly creating your reality. In order to get up to choice you must come up to source—into the creative realm of your beingness. At that level of awareness choice is so because you said so, and your word is law in your universe!

We knew that graduation was near when Victor came up before our last break to, as we thought, mechanically remind us of our "break" agreements: THIS IS NOT A DINNER BREAK. THERE WILL BE NO FOOD. THE BATHROOMS ARE LOCATED. . . . But wait a minute—instead he pulled a switch. He gave us a totally nonsensical instruction, roughly the equivalent of a drill sergeant marching his troops into a wall.

Then he broke into an ear-to-ear grin—Victor had finally taken off his mask, and there stood a real person. We knew at that point we had passed!

The training officially ended when Hal, who some time ago had taken his mask off, revealed to us that in fact we were the ones who had been "training" him. He thanked us for that as he stepped off the stage and down from his role as trainer.

Then the floodgates opened and in rushed a sea of *est* graduates, all of whom had come to "be" with us. At that point there was nothing to do but savor the moment and celebrate—so we did!

Notes

1. Luke Rhinehart, *The Book of est* (New York: Rinehart and Winston, 1976), p. 30.

2. Ibid., p. 33.

3. Ibid.

4. Ibid., pp. 44–45.

5. Ibid., p. 125.

6. Ibid., p. 129.

7. Ibid., p. 165.

8. Ibid., p. 169.

9. Ibid., p. 172.

10. Ibid., p. 173.

11. Ibid., p. 175.

12. Ibid., p. 177.

13. Ibid., p. 193.

14. Ibid., p. 194.

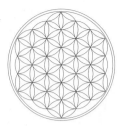

11

THE INHIBITORS

*Immortality will be given to those who unravel
the ignorance of their youth.* —Ancient Scriptures

While *est* was teaching people to keep their agreements, I would soon discover that Leonard Orr was teaching people to break them. That is, he was teaching how to break agreements we have unwittingly and unconsciously entered into—what he called being at the effect of the birth-death cycle.

The information from *est* is very powerful —it is complete unto itself, and it has the ability to transform your life. Yet for me it was never an end, only a beginning. I am using it here likewise as a foundation for what I really want to get to.

When I first met Leonard as I described in Chapter Two, I went to hear about money. Yet he began the evening talking about breathing. "Breathing," I wondered, "what's that got to do with anything? I came here to get my money case handled—let's get on with it!"

Later I would discover that the answer to my question was "Everything!" But at the time I had no idea—I thought I knew how to breathe, and I figured everyone else did too.

Rebirthing, as it turns out, is the single most important thing I have learned.

Rebirthing is an ancient technique—at least so my intuition tells me. There is a book entitled *Rebirthing According to Spirit*.[1] The entire book is channeled, and one of the channeled entities, Mother Mary, tells how rebirthing is a process that "was practiced by the Essenes . . . many thousands of years ago, even before the Master Jesus came onto this planet."[2] Another of the channeled entities, Cochise, says, "There is one who is known as Thoth, who is the vibration of the Atlantean, who is one of the master spirits that brought the whole process of rebirthing into knowingness, or into material form."[3]

Drunvalo never specifically mentioned the type of breathing Thoth did, but he did say that Thoth had to spend two hours a day breathing for 52,000 years, or he would die. I don't know if this information is true or not, but I do find it at least symbolically striking.

Anyway, Leonard Orr is the modern-day founder of rebirthing. He fills that role almost certainly for two basic reasons: first, because he had the most difficult birth imaginable, and second, because he is far ahead of his time.

According to Leonard:

> My mother had her first three children—girls—almost exactly eighteen months apart. Then she decided she had enough children. In spite of this decision she had three more . . . I was the last. An unwanted child after my mother had held the decision to have no more children for twelve years.
>
> Through rebirthing I have remembered a lot. I have remembered coming into her womb and feeling excited about being back in the physical universe. But my joy soon turned into trouble when I discovered I was an unwelcome guest. When my mother found out I was there during the second or third month of pregnancy,

she was very upset. This is when my miseries began in this life. Later, I concluded that the only way I could please my mother was to disappear—to kill myself. I tried to hang myself on my umbilical cord. It was an unsuccessful attempt. I was a breach birth with the cord wrapped around my neck three times. At birth I came as close to dying as is possible without actually dying. The cord was around my neck so tight, that the doctor decided to pull me out by my legs far enough to cut the umbilical cord, he then pushed me back in, turned me around and pulled me out with forceps. I have relived much of my womb life, birth and infancy during my rebirthing healing process. I never felt welcome in my family and most of the time I still don't.

...My birth was a long one. I remember the suffocation. I remember my mother's shame at having her legs spread. At one point in 1977 I had a rash around my neck in three stripes, which was a physiological memory of the umbilical cord.[4]

Rebirthing is a two-stage process. The first is learning to breathe energy (life force energy, or *prana*) as well as air. The second is, in Leonard's words, "to unravel the birth-death cycle, and to incorporate the body and mind into the conscious life of the Eternal Spirit, to become a conscious expression of the Eternal Spirit."[5]

Most people can have a thorough experience of what it means to breathe prana as well as air in their first guided rebirthing session. And they can learn to do it for themselves after ten or so sessions with a well-trained rebirther.

It should be noted that prana is even more vital for our existence than air. We cannot exist for even one second without it. While we do take in prana along with the air we breathe, we do it unconsciously, and we breathe it in infinitesimally small amounts—just enough to keep the body alive but not enough to even begin to experience its incredible healing capabilities. It is like a homeopathic microdose.

"Rebirthing as unraveling the birth-death cycle takes longer than learning to breathe energy. . . . It involves personal liberation from birth trauma, infancy consciousness, family patterns, and the death urge. It involves mind and body mastery."[6]

In order to understand what is meant by this, we need to dig deeper and get an understanding of these inhibiting factors that have literally kept us asleep and unconscious for far too long.

Birth Trauma

Birth trauma is caused by the sudden and unexpected shock of going from the comforting confines of the womb into an environment that is totally unfamiliar.

In the womb all of our needs were met. We lived in safety and comfort and there was no struggle. Then our bodies became too big for their containers and suddenly we were forced down a passageway that seemed too small.

This experience was painful, frightening, and distressing for both the mother and the infant. Then we found ourselves in a hostile world that was cold, bright, and noisy.

What we really needed was to be shown that the outside world is safe, and it is a far more interesting place with infinitely more possibilities than the womb. Unfortunately, we were shown the opposite—not because the people in the delivery room were evil, but because each of them had their own unresolved birth traumas, which were transmitted to the infant in the form of fear, tension, and urgency. So rather than safety and trust, the setting was one of fear. Out of fear comes ignorance. This has led to a set of false assumptions regarding the newborn.

It has been assumed that babies feel nothing during birth. We have concluded that since they don't have fully developed senses, they aren't capable of intense emotions. They have no conscious awareness, they can't see or hear, so how could an infant feel pain? We assume that because they can't speak, they can't communicate or express themselves. Yet the newborn is crying out for help. It is we who do not listen. We seem blind to the possibility that the baby is suffering.

So while it is assumed the baby feels nothing, in fact, he feels everything. "Birth is a tidal wave of sensation, surpassing anything we can imagine. A sensory experience so vast we can barely conceive of it."[7]

The delivery room is set up for the convenience of the attending physicians, beginning with the bright lights aimed at the mother's pelvic area. The baby is very sensitive to light and able to perceive it while still in the womb. The first thing the newborn sees are bright floodlights. The infant is blinded by the light; then several drops of a burning liquid are put into his or her eyes.

The baby is also able to hear in the womb, and of course the impulses are muted, but in the delivery room they are not. So the first sounds the newborn hears amount to a thunderous explosion of noise—too much for tender eardrums.

The temperature in the womb is about ninety-eight degrees Fahrenheit, and the temperature in the delivery room is about seventy degrees. This means the nude, wet newborn experiences a sudden thirty-degree drop in temperature. That is the equivalent of taking a hot bath and then running outside. This "temperature trauma" remains in the body in a suppressed state, and it is most likely the cause of colds. This suppressed trauma can be observed when people in the process of healing this memory go through dramatic temperature changes during their first few rebirthing sessions.

Furthermore, the infant is not given an opportunity to make an easy transition with its breath. We breathed one way in the womb and, because the umbilical cord is cut immediately, we are forced to learn to breathe outside the womb instantly, in a do-or-die situation.

Air striking the lungs for the first time results in unbelievable searing pain. Yet the infant must breathe—there is no alternative. The cord has been cut.

Breathing then becomes subconsciously associated with the pain, fear, and panic of the first breath. This results in perpetual anxiety and feelings of urgency. In order to keep this suppressed, we learn to breathe in a very shallow manner.

Tremendous damage was done to our breathing mechanism at birth. Fortunately, it can be healed. This in great measure is what the first ten rebirthing sessions are about. Once the memories associated with the first breath are integrated, full and free breathing is the result.

Often, the infant is held upside down and spanked to expedite the process of draining the amniotic fluid from the lungs in order to facilitate breathing. This is extremely traumatic to the newborn, often resulting in chronic back problems.

After all this, what the infant most needs is to be reunited with his or her mother. Instead the newborn is whisked away and placed in a little box in the nursery. The baby is left alone, trembling with terror, hiccuping, and choking.

Such is the trauma of birth. Having considered all this, the fact remains that it's over and you survived it! So what's the significance of birth? In many ways, it's the conclusions we all made about life as a result of this early experience. These conclusions have become our lens through which we see life, and they continue to produce results in present time until they are unraveled.

Some of these conclusions are: 1) fear of change, or fear of the unknown—integrating the fear of change associated with birth makes it easier to go through changes in life; 2) our aliveness hurts people—going through the birth canal activates our mother's birth trauma; this in turn causes her to tense up and shut down, which causes her fear and pain; and the infant might conclude that it was his or her fault; 3) pain follows pleasure—the pleasure of the womb is followed by the pain of birth; 4) you can't trust people, they hurt you; 5) the world is hostile; 6) you have to struggle to survive; and 7) breathing causes pain.

The Parental Disapproval Syndrome

First I want to be clear that this discussion is not about blame. Blame always evades responsibility. It locks energy in place and ensures the continuance and abundance of what you said you did not want.

Parenthood is probably the most difficult job on the planet for which there is no proper training. All parents have done the best they could, given what they had to work with.

The point is, all parents are at the effect of what I call a pattern—that is, unconscious, repetitive behavior handed down from generation to generation. Our parents disapproved of us because they were disapproved of by their parents, because they were disapproved of by their parents, etc. . . . As you can see, this quickly becomes a vicious circle. Does it sound familiar?

Parents manipulate their children because they were manipulated by their parents, and so on. They use discipline (control) to keep their children in line. The message to the children is that they are not okay the way they are—love and approval are conditional, and must be earned.

Our parents experienced disapproval as children. They resented it, but they suppressed their feelings because they didn't have a big enough body or vocabulary to get even, and they had probably already learned that it wasn't okay to express anger. The only thing they could do was more of what was disapproved of, which only caused more disapproval. This often led to punishment—physical abuse, verbal abuse, being ignored, being isolated, or being thrown a fierce glance.

At a certain point, the children gave up and decided they couldn't win. They decided to surrender their divine authority in the name of following instructions. Most people have been following instructions ever since. They were invalidated by their parents the same way their parents were invalidated by their parents, etc.

They also may have concluded that there was something wrong with them, that they were bad, and these children may have begun to disapprove of themselves. We all have inside us a parent and a child, so one's inner parent can be used to disapprove of the inner child. We carry out the whole cycle in our own minds and bodies without any further input.

At the point at which approval becomes a need, children begin to experience anxiety as a result of fear of disapproval. This is based on the assumption that our self-worth depends on what others think of us (or what the "others" inside us think of us).

When approval becomes a need or an addiction, rather than a preference, a person becomes a conformist, spending his or her life conforming to parents and other authority figures in order to earn their approval. A common pattern that emerges then is the need-obligate syndrome. The person has decided. . . . he can't do what he wants to get what he needs, and since others have what he needs, he is obligated to do whatever others want. He is then dependent upon others and must perform some unpleasant task to earn the love and approval he so desperately needs. Approval is a need that must be earned.

The other side of the coin is a rebel. He has given up on approval and spurns it.

There is ultimately no difference between a rebel and a conformist. They are both at the effect of the same thing. Rebels are simply conformists who have given up hope of getting what they need, so they cover up that need with a rebel act.

A common pattern that emerges from rebel consciousness is called "failing to get even," especially if your parents put pressure on you to succeed. The decision made here is: "Since you were such terrible parents, I'll get even with you. I'll fail." So you fail in jobs and relationships, or if something starts going right you find a way to sabotage it, because if you succeeded, you would have to admit they did a good job in raising you.

You may also play this out by attempting to be far more successful than your parents were, but because it is based on getting even, it is success without satisfaction.

The problem here is that you never really get *even enough*. In fact, it becomes a game of one-upmanship, at which point failure becomes what your life is about. You are the one who fails to get even because getting even is itself an act of failure. Only giving up the game releases you.

Since parents are your fundamental relationship, anything unresolved between you will come up in your other relationships. In fact, your life is about your incompletion with your parents—you will find yourself being shaped by, dominated by, and limited by this incomplete relationship.

You will find yourself creating "substitute parents," where "you tend to recreate their *personalities* as closely as possible in your other relationships."[8] That means you will probably discover at some point that you married your mother or father, or your boss is your father. So in order to make it with your mate or at work, you first must complete your relationship with your parents.

Also, "you tend to recreate the *kind of relationships* you had with your parents in your other relationships."⁹ You will tend to find a partner who treats you the way your parents treated you, and you will tend to act out your parents' roles in your current relationships.

Then when you have children, you will have finally gone one full turn on the vicious cycle. You have finally found someone on whom you can take out your suppressed hostility. And around and around it goes unless you end the cycle.

Notes

1. Denis W. Ouellette, *Rebirthing According to Spirit* (San Diego, CA: Pacific Beach Printing, 1982).

2. Ibid., p. 14.

3. Ibid., p. 5.

4. Leonard Orr, *The Story of Rebirthing* (Chico, CA: Inspiration University), pp. 3–4.

5. Ibid., p. 1.

6. Ibid., p. 2.

7. Frederick Leboyer, *Birth Without Violence* (New York: Alfred A. Knopf, 1976), p. 15.

8. Sondra Ray, *Loving Relationships* (Berkeley, CA: Celestial Arts, 1980), p. 32.

9. Ibid.

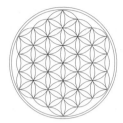

12

REBIRTHING

The mind and the breath are the King and Queen of human consciousness.   —Leonard Orr

History

Leonard Orr developed rebirthing over a thirteen-year period as a result of his experiences of birth memories. These memories began in 1962, when he suddenly couldn't get out of his bathtub. He says he stayed there for two hours before he had enough strength to get out.

Leonard had numerous rebirthing experiences between 1962 and 1975. One of the most dramatic that he tells about occurred in 1973 when, as the result of a terrible headache, he intuitively decided to get down on the floor on his hands and knees with his head down so it touched the floor. He then had a birth memory and the pain immediately stopped.

I will continue with the history of rebirthing in Leonard's own words:

> In 1974 I gave a spiritual psychology seminar. I talked about my birth memories and most of the people attending wanted to have birth memories too. I told

them to get into their bathtubs and sit there until they felt it was time to get out. Then, to stay in the tub thirty minutes to an hour longer. The feeling that we must get out is an urgency barrier. Every time we sit through an urgency barrier we get a fantastic realization about ourselves and we learn about another program that is controlling us. This was the first technique of Rebirthing: to just sit and meditate in the bathtub through an urgency barrier.

Most of the people in the seminar group tried this experiment and had such powerful emotional releases that they wished someone had been there to talk with them about what was happening to them. I volunteered. I experimented with Rebirthing people this way. It was very powerful.

Later I got the idea of using a snorkel and nose clips in a hot tub. When I put people into the water, they were in a womb-like environment and they instantly regressed to birth and prenatal states of consciousness. They did not just have memories, they regressed to a psycho-physical state. It was a complete spiritual, mental and physical experience. People had a completed energy cycle which was an integrated healing experience. I stayed with each person until they felt peace. They experienced the peace that surpasses all understanding. . . .

In 1975, after giving hundreds of hot tub Rebirths, I noticed people having a "healing of the breath" experience. I realized their breathing mechanism was totally transformed and their mind-body-spirit relationship was forever transformed. This healing took place after several sessions—when they felt safe enough to relive the moment of their first breath. Most people feel fear during this moment, so they have to feel safe to reach it.

They all breathed in a certain rhythm. It was a connected rhythm in which the inhale was merged with the exhale in one breath. It was the unity of Being experienced physiologically. It was the merging of the inner breath—life energy—with the outer breath—air and the breathing mechanism.

From the very beginning it was my goal to make people spiritually self-sufficient with Energy Breathing. That is, to give them enough sessions until they could Rebirth themselves.

Next I experimented with this connected breathing rhythm without the water and found that it was much better to do ten one- to two-hour Connected Breathing sessions out of the water before giving people a session in a hot tub with nose clips and a snorkel. Dry Rebirthing was born. This made it possible for Rebirthing to become a mass movement. Getting in a hot tub, nude except for a snorkel and nose clips, and reliving your birth, was a little esoteric for most people. But now all people had to do was lie down and breathe and they could have the most marvelous experience of their life.[1]

In their first rebirthing session, most people can learn not only how to breathe prana, but the connected breathing rhythm. In their first ten sessions with a good rebirther they gain a thorough experience of what it means to breathe energy or prana as well as air. Training and repetition take them through the landscape often enough that they become able to navigate on their own. Like fish transform into reptiles, they are now full-fledged land-breathers.

The key is being with a well-trained breathing guide with whom you feel safety and trust. That can best be illustrated by my telling you of my early rebirthing experiences.

My History

I discovered rebirthing purely by accident. As I indicated in the previous chapter, I initially heard of it when I first met Leonard Orr. But I wasn't there to breathe. I was there for a money seminar, so it blew right over me, literally and figuratively.

Then in February of 1979 I took a weekend workshop on relationships co-led by two friends of mine. At one point they told us we were going to do the "breakthrough process." The previous weekend they had taken Sondra Ray's Loving Relationships Training (LRT). In the LRT, there is a group rebirthing session given one evening. That was their introduction to rebirthing. The entire group lies down on the floor and is guided through the process together. It is a shared journey through individual experiences. Usually there is one guide for every ten to fifteen rebirthees. Some have a satisfactory session and some don't. It works best when the participants are all experienced in rebirthing.

So we were going to do the "breakthrough process." They didn't even call it rebirthing. They were in no way qualified to do this; they had little more than a clue as to what they were doing.

They described and demonstrated what they called a connected breathing rhythm and then told us to lie down and begin breathing in that manner. They offered no other explanation. Their description instantly triggered a red alert in my mind. I knew it would cause hyperventilation, and I *knew* that was dangerous.

So I lay down on the floor along with the rest of the group (there were about ten of us), and because of my extensive belief system about hyperventilation, I decided *not* to breathe that way. Then my friend, the co-leader, looked at me and saw I wasn't breathing. Of course, he instructed me to breathe as directed. I said, "No, it's hyperventilating and that's dangerous." He said, "No, it's OK, breathe."

I decided to breathe only when he was watching me. Since there were ten of us, he would only be noticing me about ten percent of the time.

When he watched I breathed. Of course, I was fighting it and resisting it all the way. It felt scary and awful. The moment he looked away, I stopped. And so it went for what seemed like an eternity. I breathed just enough to make myself sick. I felt dizzy and nauseated. It took me a few hours to recover. So breathing is not just a straightforward automatic thing. Because of our births and what we are carrying around with us, it takes training and an able guide. Otherwise you are playing with dynamite.

One month later, I found myself in a two-day rebirthing workshop given by two qualified rebirthers. By now I had heard from others that rebirthing was a powerful and useful healing process, so I did want to learn about it despite my previous experience. I felt that since it would be led by two professional rebirthers, I would be in good hands but, in fact, this experience was even worse than the first one because my fears and resistance from a month prior were so strong. This shows how fear and poor breathing reinforce each other even when there is an opportunity to escape the cycle.

The first day began with a demonstration session. We were just to sit and observe the process of a person being rebirthed. It was long and boring, and most of us quickly lost interest.

About an hour into the session many of us had reconvened in the kitchen. We were in there having a good old time when the male trainer came in and, in *est* fashion, informed us of our agreement to be in the other room in support of the rebirthing session. It seemed stupid and pointless; it looked to me as though the person was just sleeping through most of the session, but nevertheless, in we went. I learned nothing from watching.

Then it was time to pair up and exchange guided sessions. It turned out to be the blind leading the blind. I knew nothing and my partner was equally unprepared.

We were instructed to breathe as fully as we could, through our mouths because we get more air that way. That is the only instruction I remember. They may have explained exactly and perfectly how to do a session, but if they did, I didn't hear it.

My session lasted for three hours and, as I said, it was worse than my first experience a month earlier. The mouth breathing immediately recreated a full-tilt memory of my frequent bouts with car sickness as a young child. I fought and resisted as long as I could until I could hold it no more. I threw up. From there, it only got worse.

The session finally ended not because I was complete (I wasn't—I felt like a scrambled egg; it took me hours to recover), but because everyone else had finished at least an hour earlier. It was time for one final process before we went home.

Then, after all that, they told us we were now rebirthers and could go home and practice with our partners or spouses. Like a dummy, I believed them. I went home and did just that!

My girlfriend at the time and I practiced with each other a few times. Since we knew nothing, we were only able to recreate the terror and torture of my previous two experiences. We weren't infinitely stupid though, and finally we decided to give up and either learn how to do it right, or put it to bed forever.

My point here is simple. If you want to learn rebirthing, go to a well-trained, qualified rebirther with whom you feel a sense of safety and trust. Go to someone who is clear on their purpose—to act as a guide and to allow and trust your breath and your life energy to do the session. Also, find someone who knows that his or her job is to make the rebirther obsolete; his or her job is to teach you how to do it for yourself.

Rebirthing and the Three Notions of *est*

Now let's look again at the three notions of *est* and apply them to the rebirthing process.

Again, the first notion is: You are perfect, but there are barriers preventing you from experiencing and expressing your perfection.

These barriers come mainly from birth trauma and parental conditioning, as detailed in the previous chapter. They literally live in the body in the form of stuck energy, held in place by shallow breathing.

Rebirthing goes right to this stuck energy. If you have a glass of water with a layer of mud on the bottom (old stuck energy), and you begin pouring in a constant stream of fresh water (new energy), the first thing that happens is the mud is stirred up and the water becomes muddy. If you continue pouring in the fresh water, eventually all the mud (old stuck energy) will get flushed out and you will be left with a glass of fresh, pure water (new energy).

In rebirthing, prana or life-force energy is the equivalent of the fresh water, and the old stuck energy from birth and parental conditioning is the mud. We are talking about a three-step process here. When the layer of mud is just sitting at the bottom of the glass, you have suppression. When it is being stirred around by the flow of fresh water, you have a state called activation. It can manifest as fear, as you might remember from the earlier chapters of this book. Integration or completion is the state in which all the mud has been flushed out and you are left with a glass of pure, fresh water.

So, to get back to rebirthing: The old stuck energy held in place by shallow breathing is the state of suppression. In this state we are able to function, sort of. It's just that our lives are shaped by, formed by, and molded by this stuck energy, in ways that limit our full expression. This stuck energy also creates tension and unpleasant symptoms in the body, eventually leading to disease and ultimately death.

When you begin the rebirthing breath—that is, pulling on the inhale, relaxing on the exhale and breathing in a connected or circular manner with no pause—the inhale merges into and becomes the exhale, and the exhale merges into and becomes the inhale. As you continue this, you begin to feel a tingling and vibrating sensation in various parts of or throughout your body. Also, a layer of the old stuck energy begins to get stirred up, arising from suppression into a state of activation.

In medical terms, this is known as hyperventilation. It is defined as over-breathing and is considered to be a disease. In his book *Breath Awareness* Leonard compiled a list of symptoms associated with the hyperventilation syndrome. They include:

Rapid breathing
Forced or heavy breathing
Involuntary breathing
Difficulty with breathing, including asthma attacks
Tingling or vibrating sensations in hands or feet
Choking
Tetany (a medical term for temporary paralysis or cramps)
Light-headedness or dizziness
Hysterical crying
Irrational feelings of fear or terror
Fainting
Out-of-body experiences
Temporary insanity

Localized feelings of extreme pressure on body parts
Strong energy flows
Fluctuating body temperature
Extreme sweating or inconsolable cold
Confusion
Claustrophobia
Headache
Body rushes
Full-body orgasmic feelings
Spiritual or religious visions
Dramatic telepathic experiences
Nausea
Dryness of mouth
Buzzing or ringing in the ears
Birth memories or dream-like states
Euphoria and blissful states
Color fantasies and vivid color perception
Muscle spasms including epileptic-type seizures
Death and resurrection experiences[2]

Hyperventilation is not a disease. It is a healing in process to counteract the fact that you have subventilated all your life. It is the healing in process for the damage done to your breathing mechanism during birth.

One of the hyperventilation symptoms most people go through is a phenomenon called tetany. This is a temporary involuntary tightening or paralysis of the joints, usually in the hands and face. It can be viewed as your body's way of showing you how much you have been "holding on" all your life. The keys to getting through it lie in the second and third notions of *est*. The second notion is: Resistance leads to persistence. In rebirthing, this dynamic is intensified. If you resist the paralysis, you can lock your entire body up in tetany to the point where it feels as though it will never go away.

The way out is always *through*, which brings us to the third notion: Recreate equals disappear. If you can allow yourself to have a thorough experience of what you would normally tend to resist, the tetany will disappear. You need to "tune" to it and allow yourself to feel it fully. Then it will disappear.

I learned this truth, you might say, the hard way. I was at Campbell Hot Springs in May of 1980, and felt I was advanced enough to go into a hot tub and rebirth myself unassisted. Rebirthing in warm water is a very advanced form, not to be attempted until you have had at least ten successful "dry" sessions. In my case, I had and I thought I was ready.

Just a few minutes into the session my entire body became paralyzed. I could not move a muscle. For the most part, I was petrified—the possibility of drowning was *very* real. But there was a small part of me, a very small part—maybe it was only one cell in my big toe—but nevertheless this small part of me was actually getting off on this experience. I had very little time to make a decision, so I intuitively decided to go with the part of me that was enjoying the experience. As I did the paralysis instantly lifted. What had been a terrifying experience suddenly became a totally freeing and exhilarating experience—and a very powerful lesson. This is emotional-body clearing at its most dramatic. We all have times when we need to find the one part of ourselves, however tiny, that is not involved in fear.

I knew the three notions of *est*, but at that point I only knew them conceptually. Now I was given an involuntary opportunity to relearn them experientially.

Regarding the second notion, it is well to remember that when the mind thinks it is the self, it thinks it needs all its old stuff for survival. Remember, the tape it is playing contains a thorough record of how you survived.

The key here is awareness, which leads to safety and trust. A good rebirther can provide this with certainty: He or she is a companion, a protector, a psychic guide, and a mirror. I have often compared learning rebirthing to learning to fly an airplane. If you want to learn to fly a plane, I doubt the best course of action would be to get in, sit in the cockpit, and take off—solo. It would seem beneficial to learn from an experienced pilot who could teach you in a setting of safety and trust how to get off the ground and stay aloft. Then after a few lessons, you would be on your own.

The same is true with rebirthing. Trying it out initially on your own can bring up symptoms that literally terrify you, and you can easily get stuck in them. That was certainly true for me. I developed fears, defenses, and body armor that turned me into a pretty tough case. Breath had become my enemy and my tomb.

If you are with someone you trust and are properly prepared, you can go right through it. It doesn't have to be a torturous experience like mine. I just seem to like to do things the hard way. It takes a pole shift—or the threat of one—to wake me up. But once I'm awake I'm ready to take on asteroids and demons both.

A good rebirther will teach you that the breathing rhythm is, as Leonard used to say, "not a discipline, rather it is an inspiration." It is about giving up control. Most people's breathing is totally controlled; they push the exhale out, pause, and then let the inhale in almost as an afterthought. One gives up control, but only to their own body, their inner wisdom.

Rebirthing is oddly comparable to hitting a golf ball. Volumes have been written on the mechanics of the swing, and it's just that—mechanics. The point is you need to understand all of it well enough to let it go and be in the rhythm or the flow of the swing. At that point you are one with the swing—you become the swing.

The same is true for the breath. When you let go and trust the breath, you discover the true control of full, free breathing. You discover that you are being breathed by the infinite intelligence contained in the breath, and it knows exactly what to do.

At that point you are effortlessly relaxing and tuning to the process. Just continue to let yourself feel the symptoms without judgment. That lets you have a thorough experience of them, which in turn leads to their disappearance.

The session is complete when the layer of old stuck energy has been replaced by new energy. It usually takes one to two hours.

Intention

Now, the most important aspect of all this is you. Rebirthing is only a tool; the question is how you use it. The proper tools in the hands of a skilled carpenter can result in a beautiful piece of furniture. The same tools in the hands of the Three Stooges will produce something else entirely.

What I'm getting at is your intention to produce the desired result in the first place. We live in a free-will universe, so you must choose, and the choice must be yours—it must come from you. It won't work if you are doing it to please someone else, or if you are doing it because some "expert" recommended it. The act must be because you said so, period.

Out of choice comes intention to produce the desired result. Your intention must be one hundred percent.

For every condition you have that you say you don't want, on some level—usually a very unconscious level—you do want it and you chose it in the first place. That means there is a payoff somewhere. You will let go of the condition when there is no more value in keeping it around, i.e., when you have identified the payoff and with one hundred percent intention decided to let it go.

I will give an example. Let's suppose that as a child you normally didn't receive much attention. You just went along and did okay in school and did your chores and were pretty much unnoticed. Then suppose you got sick, really sick, when you were in bed for an extended period of time, and all of a sudden, people noticed. They waited on you, took care of your needs, kept asking how you felt, told you stories and spent time with you, etc. You may have concluded that sick was better.

So now as an adult, you may have a pattern of sickness, but it no longer serves you as it did when you were a child. In order to let go of the unwanted condition, you must let go of the payoff. Your intention, in other words, must be one hundred percent.

Out of one hundred percent intention comes responsibility. You must step up to ownership. You created the condition whether you understand it or not. It is the only way to be in your full power. If you can accept that you one hundred percent created the unwanted condition, then you can one hundred percent create it any way you want. It is simple, but that is why it is so hard to see. People are too caught up in a web of complications to be able to claim the obvious and get on with things. They prefer their own melodramas.

When you are completely willing to let go and give up the limiting condition, you will find yourself in a state of natural knowingness. This natural knowingness is something we all have. We only need to claim it. From it comes certainty and healing. Limiting conditions cannot exist in that state.

Out of the foundation of safety and trust, relax and breathe and tune to whatever you are feeling, so you can feel it fully. When you are able to feel it fully, you are recreating it and it will disappear.

Notes

1. Leonard Orr, *The Story of Rebirthing* (Chico, CA: Inspiration University), pp. 6–8.

2. Leonard Orr, *Breath Awareness* (Sierraville, CA: Inspiration University, 1988), p. 18.

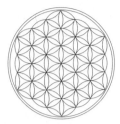

13

INTEGRATION

Emotions are energy in motion. We need them, and we need to have a healthy relationship with them. But we have all been emotionally abused to some degree, and have learned as a result that at least some of our emotions are not okay.

For example, when young were you really allowed to feel and express your anger when your needs were being violated? Most likely you were told, "Never act like that again," or "Don't you ever talk to me like that again! What's wrong with you? Shame on you!" So you more than likely learned at an early age that anger wasn't okay.

Sadness makes insecure parents feel as though they're not creating a happy home for their children. You may have been told, "Quit crying, you big sissy—what's the matter with you?" or maybe "Stop crying or I'll give you something to cry about!" In this way you learned you couldn't be sad.

Being afraid may have disturbed your parents. You may have been laughed at, or your fear may have been minimized by being told there was nothing to fear. So you learned that fear wasn't okay. This can be especially true for boys who are often called a "sissy" and told to "act like a man."

It may not have been okay even for you to feel joy, given that most parents unwittingly prevent their children from having higher self-esteem than they do. So you may have learned that you have no right to be happy or enthusiastic.

What this means is that if you were told you were wrong, bad, stupid, or crazy for feeling what you felt, then you learned on a very deep level that there was something wrong with you for feeling the way you did. In other words, you were shamed for feeling your emotions, and according to author John Bradshaw, shaming is the most damaging assault on your self-esteem because it has no boundaries. Your whole being is affected by shame.

Bradshaw's excellent book on shame is called *Healing the Shame That Binds You.*[1] Much of my information on shame came from a bootleg audio tape of a talk Bradshaw gave in Houston, Texas, probably circa 1985. While I can't tell you much more about this tape's availability, I can tell you that it has been very instrumental in putting me in touch with my suppressed shame. You see, I came from a shame-based family too.

This has not been an easy book for me to write in the sense that it is about my personal journey of discovery. Just because I write books and have taught this material for seventeen years doesn't mean I have mastered every aspect of it. The act of writing this book has set in motion a very concentrated form of the process—in other words, anything I am holding onto that is less pure than what I am writing about will come to my attention. Then I get to integrate it. I can't write about something until it has integrated, so I can't write any faster than that.

Most of the shaming in my family came in the form of emotional abuse. I have integrated a lot of it in recent weeks, and it is very freeing. One of my concerns about writing on these topics was, "What will my parents think?" Then I realized, again, this is not about blame. My parents were shame-based too; they were just passing it on. That's the nature of a pattern. It is multi-generational.

Then I realized that by writing this I am breaking the pattern, and in so doing, giving them the same opportunity. In fact, everyone who reads this is being given that chance, and that is bigger than my concern—much bigger!

So if you experienced emotional abuse, you have emotional problems to some degree, and the emotions are bound with shame. After a while you don't feel shame anymore because you have internalized it, and now you *are* it! You have learned on a very deep level that you are worthless, that you can't trust your feelings or perceptions, that you always get it wrong because you are wrong—not because you made a mistake, but you *are* a mistake.

You may have noticed these unresolved emotions don't just dissolve. They live in the body in the form of stuck energy, held in place by shallow breathing. Furthermore, because they create unpleasant sensations in the body you develop body armor and withdraw awareness from your body. You then internalize the emotion through denial, avoidance, or self-blame, or you externalize by acting out or blaming others. Neither way ever produces emotional resolution.

Integration comes from awareness and acceptance of what you are feeling so you can allow yourself to have a thorough experience of it. It is applying the third notion of *est*. This works even if you don't use rebirthing. If you do use rebirthing, you speed up the process and make it infinitely more powerful. The natural function of prana is to bring to your attention anything you have been holding onto that is less pure than prana, i.e., stuck energy. Then, if you continue to breathe, the stuck energy gets replaced by new energy.

Now let's look at emotions, beginning with sadness, and how they integrate. Let's be very dramatic here and suppose you just lost your best friend. The one person you could count on and confide in just died. That means you need to go through the feelings of sadness and grief, and you need to feel them fully. When you have had a thorough experience, these feelings will integrate. When they do, you are left with gratitude for having had what you had with this person, the memories, etc.

Fear integrates into excitement, exhilaration, and alertness. I will give some examples: In my first rebirthing experience in a hot tub my entire body went into tetany, as I described above. Because I went with it, I allowed myself to have a thorough experience of the fear, and it became absolutely exhilarating. Another example would be a roller coaster ride. For a person stuck in fear, it would be an awful experience. For another, it could be very exciting and exhilarating. Fear also integrates into alertness. From integrating my fear of driving, I became a very alert driver, always aware of the traffic and road conditions, yet calm and relaxed.

Anger integrates into determination, which facilitates your effort to get your needs met. Guilt and shame integrate into innocence and a more complete awareness of your natural divinity. Since all your emotions are bound with shame, there will be an integration of shame every time you integrate an emotion. Integrating shame-bound emotions is one of the keys in reclaiming your child-like innocence, which is essential in the process of reconnecting with your higher self and your natural divinity.

Shame severs us from experiencing our natural divinity. If you believe that you *are* a mistake, how could you ever be divine? Even if you could allow yourself to feel your natural divinity, you would find a way to sabotage it, since you believe that you are fundamentally flawed. You would have to.

By the way, you do know how to integrate emotions and you have done it many times. You wouldn't be alive if you hadn't. Every time you have gotten the monkey off your back or gotten something off your chest, you have integrated something. All I am trying to do is nail it to the wall for you.

Notes

1. John Bradshaw, *Healing the Shame That Binds You* (Deerfield Beach, FL: Health Communications, Inc., 1988).

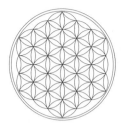

14

FORGIVENESS

Forgiveness is the master erase. It is necessary in the same way that it would be necessary to clean out a closet filled with moth-bitten clothes in order to make space for a new wardrobe.

You have to let go of your old resentments and scores in order to make room for your greater good. You can't have both, so you must choose and you must do so with one hundred percent intention.

My first serious work with forgiveness was in 1981 when I was a staff member at the old Theta House in San Francisco. Another staff member, Leah Holtzman, created a very powerful seminar called "Forgiveness equals Fortune." It was so dubbed because shortly after forgiving her father, she received an unexpected gift of $10,000 from him. She was impressed by that. "Hey, this really works!" she probably thought.

That motivated her to create a seminar. I took it several times. What follows is directly from her workshop.

Definitions of Forgiveness

    . . . to cease to bear resentment against
    . . . to give up resentment against or the desire to punish
    . . . to stop being angry with

. . . to pardon, to overlook

. . . "give for" or to "replace" the ill feeling, to gain a sense of peace and harmony

. . . to give love for yourself

Forgiveness is a simple yet sometimes misunderstood word. Compiled here are some enlightened and concise statements about forgiveness.

Catherine Ponder (Famous Unity Minister)

" . . . If you have a problem you have something to forgive. Anyone who experiences pain has a need to forgive. Anyone who finds himself in unpleasant circumstances has a need to forgive. Anyone who finds himself in debt has a need to forgive. Where there is suffering, unhappiness, lack, confusion or misery of any sort, there is a need to forgive."

" . . . Resentment, condemnation, anger, the desire to 'get even' or to see someone punished or hurt, are things that rot your soul and tear down your health. You must forgive injuries and hurts of the past and present, not so much for the other person's sake as for your own."

" . . . Hurt or hate of any kind scars the soul and works an illness in the flesh. The illness will not be fully healed while you continue to remain unforgiving."

" . . . Forgiveness begins with the one who recognizes the offense. When you get the offense out of your own heart, you have forgiven. The reconciliation which you bring about within yourself will have its effect upon your brother, and there will be an automatic forgiving on his part toward you."

" . . . Genuine forgiveness is not a casual act. The word means a 'cleansing' or a blotting out of transgression. It takes time and persistence for true forgiveness to invade the subconscious levels."

" . . . You may not consciously be aware of what or whom you need to forgive in the past or present. It is not necessary that you know, though often it will be revealed to you, as you invoke forgiveness. The only requirement is that you willingly speak words of forgiveness and let those words do their cleansing work."

" . . . To forgive means to 'give for' to 'replace' the ill feeling, to gain a sense of peace and harmony again. To forgive literally means to 'give up' that which you should not have held onto in the first place."

" . . . If only one person will dare to forgive, the problem can be solved, regardless of who else is involved, and whether anyone else wants to forgive. The person who dares to forgive gains control of the situation. You may not have appeared to have any prior power to solve the problem, but suddenly there will be a change. The person who forgives will find a divine solution appearing."

" . . . You must forgive if you want to be permanently healed. Health cannot be accepted by a body that is filled with the poisons generated by unforgiveness."

" . . . When your good is delayed, that is the time to forgive. Forgiveness can sweep aside all that has delayed you in your race toward good."

" . . . The forgiving state of mind is a magnetic power for attracting good. No good thing can be withheld from a forgiving state of mind."

" . . . If Jesus had not dared to say on the cross, 'Father, forgive them for they know not what they do,' he could not have experienced resurrection."

" . . . Forgiveness is all powerful. Forgiveness heals all ills. Forgiveness makes the weak strong. Forgiveness makes the cowardly courageous. Forgiveness makes the ignorant wise. Forgiveness makes the mournful happy. Forgiveness can unblock whatever has stood between you and your good. LET IT!"

A Course in Miracles

"The unforgiving mind is full of fear and offers love no room to be itself."

"The unforgiving mind is sad without the hope of respite and release from pain."

"The unforgiving mind is torn with doubt, confused about itself and all it sees."

"The unforgiving mind is afraid to go ahead and afraid to stay."

"The unforgiving mind does not believe that giving and receiving are the same."

" . . . Without forgiveness the mind is in chains, believing in its own futility. Yet with forgiveness does the light shine through the dream of darkness, offering it hope, and giving it the means to realize the freedom that is its inheritance."

" . . . The illusion is that there is something to forgive. Those who forgive are thus releasing themselves from illusions, while those who withhold forgiveness are binding themselves to them. Forgiveness is the means by which illusions disappear."

" . . . Through your forgiveness does the truth about yourself return to your memory. Therefore, in your forgiveness lies your salvation."

" . . . Forgiveness wipes away the dreams of separation and of sin. Forgiveness sees that there was no sin; therefore releasing it."

" . . . Forgiveness sweeps away distortions and opens the hidden altar to the truth. Forgiveness stands between illusion and the truth."

" . . . Forgiveness is acquired, it is not inherent. Forgiveness must be learned."

Forgiveness Affirmations

. . . I forgive myself totally and completely.

. . . I forgive myself for past errors.

. . . As I forgive, I am forgiven.

. . . I am now willing to forgive myself and others for hurting me.

. . . As I forgive others, I forgive myself.

. . . As I forgive, I see the truth.

. . . As I forgive, my mind is released from the chains of resentment and negativity to the rewards of love and positivity.

. . . I am now willing to consider forgiving my mother/father/doctor who delivered me.

. . . I totally and completely forgive the doctor who delivered me. This affirmation is always true.

. . . I totally and completely forgive (put in person's name).

. . . I forgive (name) for (whatever you want to forgive them for).

. . . Forgiveness is my salvation.

. . . I forgive my mother/father/doctor for their ignorant behavior towards me at birth and during my childhood.

. . . I now release, renounce, forgive and free all my unpleasant past, all my imagined future, all thoughts and attitudes of separation and all human relationships into the Light or the Holy One.

. . . I freely forgive you. I loose you and let you go. It is done. It is finished forever.

. . . I fully and freely forgive. I loose and let go. I let go and let God do his perfect work of healing in my mind, body and affairs.

. . . All that has offended me, I forgive. Whatever has made me bitter, resentful, unhappy, I forgive. Within and without, I forgive. Things past, things present, things future, I forgive.

... I forgive everything and everybody who can possibly need forgiveness in my past and present. I forgive positively everyone. I am free and they are free. All things are cleared up between us now and forever.

... I forgive everything, everyone, every experience, every memory of the past or present that needs forgiveness. I forgive positively everyone. God is love and I am forgiven and governed by God's love alone. God's love is now adjusting my life. Realizing this, I abide in peace.

Forgiveness Exercises

I. Make a list of people you are willing to forgive. Next make a list of what Leah called "fortunes to receive." For each person you forgive, you create space for your greater good. Make a list of what you are willing to receive.

Conclude your list with the following affirmation: "This or something better now manifests for the good of all concerned and in divine order, for I am now willing to consciously receive all the gifts God has given me."

II. From the list of people you are willing to forgive, make a list of whatever it is that you resent about that person, are angry with that person about, are blaming that person for, and hate that person for.

This is not an intellectual exercise. To the best of your ability, get in touch with the feelings of resentment, anger, blame, and hatred. Allow yourself to feel them fully. You can do this as a written exercise or as an oral exercise—either with a partner or to yourself in the mirror.

Next, forgive the person for everything on your list. That is, go through each item on your list and either write, say it to yourself in the mirror, or say it to your partner who is being that person for you: I forgive you for _____.

Forgiveness comes much more easily when you begin to realize that no one really "did it" to you and there is no real satisfaction or redemption in revenge or showing someone up. There is no sanctuary in it either, only more vulnerability and danger. It is a classic case of false cause; those you have been blaming have just been running their multi-generational pattern on you because they were at the effect of their parental conditioning, who were at the effect of their parental conditioning, who were at the effect of theirs, etc., and you bought into it because you were at the effect of yours. Do you want to keep riding that roller coaster?

Beneath this endless cycle of effect lies the fact that we are all innocent, we are all children of the One Spirit, all under its protection. Forgiveness is a way of unraveling the ball of "false-cause" yarn, leaving you at the core of your innocence.

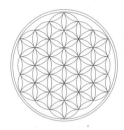

15

LIFE'S A JOY—
THEN YOU ASCEND

*Physical immortality is the only cause
you can't die for.*   — Leonard Orr

A sizable portion of the Flower of Life information came to
Drunvalo from an individual by the name of Thoth, who
52,000 years ago learned how to stay alive and, instead of
dying, went through a process called ascension. For 16,000
years he was the king of Atlantis, where his name was Chi-
quetet Arlich Vomalites. In Egypt he was Thoth. Later he
became known as Hermes of Greece. Thoth remained on
Earth in the same body until May 4, 1991. He could have left
earlier—many ascended masters have—but he was among
a small group who decided to stay. Knowing without any
doubt whatsoever that all things are interconnected and that
there is One Spirit that moves through everything, Thoth
preferred to remain here as a teacher.

In *Nothing* I told the story of how Drunvalo and Thoth
first met. Drunvalo was doing an open-eye meditation with
his alchemy teacher, who disappeared about an hour into
the meditation. Then a completely different person materialized in his place. At the time, Drunvalo had no idea who

this person was. Then on November 1, 1984, twelve years later, he appeared again. This person turned out to be Thoth. From that time until his departure on May 4, 1991, Thoth exchanged vast amounts of information with Drunvalo.

There are two points I wish to make regarding Drunvalo's interaction with Thoth.

The first point is that this was not some figment of Drunvalo's imagination, nor was it channeled. It was real. In fact, to help illustrate this, Drunvalo told a story of the one and only time he did experience Thoth channeling through him. He said he was out skiing with some friends in New Mexico, and Thoth came in and began to communicate with Drunvalo. "You know," Thoth said, "I've never done that, and it really looks like fun. Do you think, would you mind, if I got in there for a while and tried it out?" Drunvalo then checked with his inner guidance and got an okay to do it, and Thoth came in. Drunvalo said he still had the awareness of being in his body, but it was kind of like being in the back seat. Thoth was in control. So off they went. The only problem was, Thoth didn't know how to ski! So after crashing into just about everything in sight, Thoth finally decided he had enough. Drunvalo didn't see him for the rest of the day.

The second point I want to make will be in the form of a question: How did he do it? How was Thoth able to stay alive and in a body for 52,000 years? First of all, he wasn't the only one. In Lemuria, there was a couple by the name of Ay and Tyia, who not only became immortal, but they opened a school, the Naacal Mystery School, for the purpose of teaching immortality and ascension to others.

Even though we have barely, if at all, considered it, there are in fact two alternatives to physical death as we know it.

But first let's consider what happens when we do it the conventional way. The lower overtones of the fourth dimension are rather disharmonic, and that's where we go when we die—specifically to the third overtone. This is what Drun-valo says. But we do it unconsciously, so when we get there we have no memory of our lifetime here. For the past 13,000 years we have been cycling back via reincarnation, and we have been doing that unconsciously too. So when we come back here through birth, we have no memory of where we were or of our previous lifetimes.

Also, when we come back through birth, we are again at the effect of the birth-death cycle (stay tuned, I will explain what I mean) until we become conscious enough to unravel it.

The two alternatives to physical death as we know it are both a function of consciousness. The first, resurrection, is consciously moving from one world to another by dying and then reforming your light body on the other side. With the second alternative, ascension, you don't die at all; you consciously move from one world to another, taking your body with you. It is a very responsible way of leaving.

There are two main advantages with these alternatives. First, you don't stop at the third overtone. You continue until you reach the higher, harmonic overtones of the fourth dimension—either the tenth, eleventh, or twelfth. These are usually referred to as the Christ-Consciousness overtones. Second, you are able to keep your memory intact—in fact, you will never again have a break in memory.

To me, any serious talk of ascension must include not only Spirit, but the mind and the body as well. The Holy Trinity is Spirit, mind, and body. We must learn to use the mind consciously to clear out limiting thought patterns, and we must experience the body as the temple and be fully alive in it. This is the short answer to how Thoth and the other immortals have kept from dying.

It is obvious to me in my many years as a rebirther that most people are neither fully alive, nor are they fully in their bodies. You must be fully alive and in your body in order to ascend.

In the chapter entitled "Rebirthing," I discussed the hyperventilation syndrome and how hyperventilation can be a cure for sub-ventilation, which is caused by the inhibitions built into the breathing mechanism as a result of the pain, fear, terror, and urgency associated with the first breath.

In rebirthing, there is a freeing of the breath in every session, and a permanent transformation usually takes place sometime between the third and tenth session. The healing comes about as a direct result of psycho-physically reliving the moment of the first breath. In this transformation the breathing mechanism goes from exhale-oriented to inhale-oriented.

In exhale-oriented breathing, you slowly push the exhale out, and after a long pause, inhale a small amount of air—almost as an afterthought. It is literally holding your breath, and it is the only way to keep your birth trauma suppressed. In addition, exhale-oriented breathing is a death-oriented breath insofar as it fills the cells with an excess of carbon dioxide. It takes an average of seventy years to complete the job. The birth trauma by then has become a self-fulfilling prophecy.

Inhale-oriented breathing is pulling on the inhale and relaxing on the exhale and keeping them the same length. This means that your breathing becomes efficient because you are using all your energy for the inhale. You don't have to exert effort on the exhale because gravity and your natural muscle contractions will do it for you. That leaves all your life energy for the inhale, which means that you are breathing a life-oriented breath. Additionally, you are filling the cells with oxygen, which is healthy. Your cells greatly prefer oxygen to carbon dioxide.

When you are breathing efficiently, you are breathing prana and oxygen. This combination keeps the body clean—

it flushes the circulatory, nervous, and respiratory systems as well as the aura or energy body. It cleanses psychic dirt, negative mental mass, physical tension, physical illness, and emotional problems out of human consciousness. It is amazing to me that most people go through a lifespan not knowing—and not knowing that they don't know—the healing power contained in the conscious use of their breath.

There is yet another factor that keeps us from living in the experience of our full aliveness. I must confess, I've been holding out on you. Perhaps I should have included this in "The Inhibitors," but I felt it would fit better here. What I'm talking about is the unconscious death urge.

As Leonard used to say, "Unless your parents are immortal, you have inherited a death urge." Leonard is the source of all this information. That will become increasingly clear as I continue, so I will acknowledge him now. What I have done is validate this message by living it and experiencing it for the past seventeen years.

The death urge is a real psychic entity that literally can be isolated in your own mind and destroyed. It is composed of anti-life thoughts and beliefs, and it is held in place by the belief that death is inevitable and out of your control. Its purpose is to kill you, and that is exactly what it will do, unless you kill it first.

If your thoughts, feelings, and actions unerringly create your reality, then the unquestioned, unexamined death urge that you inherited as a multi-generational pattern from your parents and from the culture will become an unwitting context for your life, and it will produce its intended result.

There is tremendous power in simply questioning the inevitability of death. Consider that the source of victim consciousness might just be the belief that you have no say in the health, well-being, and destiny of your body. The ultimate victim is someone who believes it is someone or something "out there" that has control over him or her.

If you want to take control of your life, you must include the possibility that it is *you* who creates your safety and well-being and no one else. It is *you* who creates your own health and aliveness and illness, injury, accidents, as well as the death of your physical body.

So the contradiction is that since ascension is a function of full aliveness, how can you be fully alive if you haven't unraveled your death urge? If you are unaware of it, it is unconsciously producing results.

Furthermore, the more enlightened you become, the more activated the death urge becomes. Anything you are still subconsciously holding onto that is less pure than your highest thoughts is fair game to come to your attention. And since you are becoming more conscious, your thoughts are becoming more powerful and they will manifest more quickly.

So if you have never questioned death, you are unwittingly at its effect. You will probably rationalize too and conclude that since you will be meeting your maker, it must be for the highest good. If you really want to meet your maker, go for full aliveness so you can ascend!

Physical immortality is living as long as you want, and wanting to live as long as you do. It is leaving when you choose, and doing it consciously via resurrection or ascension.

Physical immortality creates a conscious context for your life fully supportive of your aliveness—one that is broad enough even to include the death urge. That means when any life-negating thought comes to your attention, you will be able to include it in a setting of awareness, safety, and trust. That in turn will allow you to relax and breathe into it so you can experience it fully in the process of letting it go. In so doing, you can unravel your death urge one thought at a time.

Leonard said that rebirthing never could have happened had he not first unraveled his death urge, which climaxed for him in 1967. From the beginning, the idea of immortality has been contained in rebirthing. Immortality creates the certainty of safety by creating a context broad enough to include anything that might come up.

After liberating himself from his death urge, Leonard became fascinated with the idea of physical immortality. But one problem he noticed was that the authors of most of the books he had read on the subject had died. He even mentioned one person, a Divine Science minister by the name of Harry Gaze, who had written a book called *How to Live Forever.* He was giving a series of lectures on the subject at the Hollywood Church of Religious Science and died on his way to the second lecture.

Leonard decided he couldn't trust these people, so he developed a new set of criteria. He decided not to believe anyone unless they were actually doing it. He arbitrarily picked three hundred years as the minimum qualifying age. This led him to India, which was the only place he knew where actual immortals hang out. (If you are interested in exploring this fact further, please refer to a five-volume set of books, *The Life and Teachings of the Masters of the Far East* by Baird T. Spalding,[1] or Leonard's forthcoming book *Breaking the Death Habit.*[2]

Leonard went to India in the spring of 1977 but didn't find any immortals. A female traveling companion did, however. She was being guided by Babaji (stay tuned), who had materialized to her twice before the trip.

After spending seven months with Babaji, she returned to California with pictures and reports. Her transformation included having been dematerialized by Babaji for a three-day tour of the universe! As a result of these shared experiences, Leonard said he immediately tuned into Babaji's energy and has had a very powerful spiritual relationship with him ever since.

Leonard was planning a trip to India in December of 1977, but because he was very busy, he decided he wasn't going to go. Then, when the time came to make his final decision, he was meditating in a friend's house in Houston, Texas, and Babaji appeared to him and stayed for three minutes. That experience changed his mind. Leonard said it made him realize how limited his thinking was. He went to India and spent a month with Babaji.

When Leonard was with Babaji he questioned him about rebirthing. This is how Leonard recounts this conversation:

> Before I met Babaji in the flesh, I had figured out that breathing in cooperation with the mind was the key to the health of the body and mind. I had concluded that the Breath of Life could be the "Fountain of Youth" and, therefore, the key to the eternal life of the body as well as the mind. Since Babaji has mastered the eternal life of the spirit, mind and body, his body, though thousands of years old, has the appearance and integrity of a young man.
>
> So, one day in January, 1978, I mustered enough courage to test my conclusions with Babaji. It took courage on my part, because if anyone on earth could invalidate my cherished logic, it would be him. I had tested my ideas upon thousands of the world's greatest minds, but he was the first genuine immortal I had met.
>
> I said: "Does rebirthing produce Mritenjaya?" . . . (which means victory over death).
>
> He said: "Rebirthing produces Mahamritenjaya.". . . (which means supreme victory over death).
>
> I said: "You mean, since prana [life force] is eternal, the body with prana is eternal?"

He said: "Of course." And walked away as if the conversation were mundane.

To me, the confirmation of my ideas, from an actual immortal, was a big deal. But to him, I concluded, it has been simple and obvious for thousands of years. To him, it was a stupid question.[3]

Leonard said he realized that Babaji was the greatest thing on the planet, and he decided to go back and spend at least one month with him every year. Every time he went, he said, it was very tempting to just stay there and forget about the rest of the world. He also said that Babaji has given him opportunities to ascend.

In the course of his yearly treks to India, Leonard has now met eight individuals who meet his minimum qualification of three hundred years in the same body. The youngest immortal master Leonard met was three hundred years old. He would not let visitors closer than fifty yards. When asked the secret of his longevity, his reply was, "Stay away from humans."

Another, Bhartriji, was given immortality by Babaji in 56 BC. At the time he was emperor of all of India, but according to Leonard, he renounced his kingdom and became a *sadhu*. A *sadhu* is a person who gives up his worldly possessions and practices spiritual purification full-time, while living off the land.

Even though he has powers of ascension, Bhartriji has maintained a local address here on planet Earth for more than two thousand years. His ashram is located in a forest reserve of one hundred square miles. It has been reported that although the reserve contains wild animals, no human has ever been attacked by them. Bhartriji is quietly doing his job.

He has a very soft, gentle, and innocent presence. Leonard said Bhartriji felt as though he had been working on himself for two thousand years, yet he has an ageless and tension-free body. The question is the same one I would have of Thoth—how do you do it? Leonard had the same question. In fact, he was looking for the common denominator. What did these eight individuals have built into their lifestyles that enables them to keep their bodies beyond a "normal" life-span?

Notes
1. Baird T. Spalding, *The Life and Teachings of the Masters of the Far East* (Marina del Rey, CA: DeVorss & Co., Publishers, 1935).

2. Leonard Orr, *Breaking the Death Habit: Bhartriji, Immortal Yogi of 2000 Years* (Berkeley, CA: Frog, Ltd., 1998).

3. Leonard Orr, *Physical Immortality, The Science of Everlasting Life* (San Francisco: Inspiration University, 1980), p. 11.

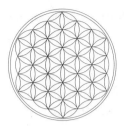

16

THE ENHANCERS

Leonard found the immortals tuning in, not out. There were no modern conveniences. No cars, televisions, microwave ovens—why, these guys aren't even on the internet! They live simply so they may simply live, in harmony with the planet and all life everywhere.

Drunvalo once gave a definition of conscious breathing that I like. He said, "You are a conscious breather when you remember your intimate connection to God and to all life everywhere on every breath." These eight immortals are conscious breathers. The breathing aspect involves the conscious inhalation of prana, while the technique of the remembrance of God's name comes primarily through the use of a mantra.

The eternal name of God is *Om Namaha Shivai* in its feminine form and *Om Namaha Shivaiya* in its masculine form. This Sanskrit phrase has been used as a mantra for millennia. Constant repetition of this mantra, called *japa*, focuses the mind on and opens the heart to God.

One of Babaji's many manifestations, according to Leonard, was Goraknath, who has trained numerous immortals. If you go to one of Goraknath's students for instruction, your first lesson will be to work continuously with the mantra

Om Namaha Shivai. Then, if you are serious, you may come back in three years for your next lesson.

Thus the remembrance of God's name is the first of the common practices. Then comes the awareness of the energy body, for the energy body is the secret to the physical body. Becoming aware of the energy body is the key to reversing the aging process and mastering the health of the body. Next comes the realization that the conscious use of the elements— earth, air, water, fire, and prana (or ether)—can cleanse the energy body or aura more efficiently than the mind. They blow away, wash away, burn away, etc., all the negative energy concentrations, for they are the physical aspects of the One Spirit.

Earth

Earth purification is developing a conscious relationship with Mother Earth; it is learning to live in harmony with Nature. It is the recognition that we are not separate from it. Standing apart, trying to conquer and control the natural world doesn't work. When we destroy Nature we destroy ourselves.

The Earth is alive. In order for you to be fully alive, you must reconnect with it—tune to it and feel it. At a certain point, it will begin to communicate back to you.

There is a huge price to pay for living in cities with all the pavement, asphalt, traffic, pollution, and electro-magnetic fields. In order to cope with it, you tune out, and in the course of doing so, you get numbed out. You lose your intuitive feel. Reconnecting with Nature is the essential aspect in getting that back.

Also included in the idea of Earth purification is movement or exercise, and food mastery. Leonard used to say that getting out of bed each morning was enough movement, and that advanced forms would begin with walking around your block every day. Yes, Leonard does have a sense of humor. I would include the possibility of hiking in Nature as often as possible, and exercising enough to keep the body toned and fit. Regarding food mastery, it is telling to note that more people in this country die as a result of overeating than undereating.

A common denominator among the five immortals in the Bible (Jesus, Moses, Enoc, Elijah, and Melchizedek) is that they each fasted for forty days with no food or water. Babaji has fasted for centuries. Leonard met a woman in Kathmandu, Nepal, who looked like she was in her thirties, yet she had fasted with no food or water for twenty years.

If that sounds too advanced for you, maybe it is well to consider the possibility of short, frequent fasts. They can teach you more than long, infrequent ones. A day per week is probably the most productive kind of fasting. In so doing, you learn discipline and a whole lot more about your mind and body, in addition to receiving the benefit of the fast. In the one-day-per-week fast, it is okay to drink juices, or even eat fruit.

At some point in your life, the idea of food mastery will almost certainly include the idea of vegetarianism. There is much I could say about this, but I will leave it to other writers. However, I will refer you to an excellent book on the subject, *Diet for a New America*,[1] by John Robbins. If you read this book, you will see how diet plays an essential role in living in harmony or disharmony with the Earth.

Air

Air purification is conscious breathing—consciously breathing life force energy or prana, that is. So when I speak of air, I am including prana.

In addition to the rebirthing information already presented, I am including below two breathing exercises. The first is twenty connected breaths, and the second is alternate nostril breathing.

Twenty Connected Breaths

The foundation of rebirthing is this simple exercise that I learned from Leonard Orr. You can do it throughout the day, whenever you feel the need. However, it is recommended that for the first week you do it only once daily:

1. Take four short breaths.
2. Then take one long breath.
3. Pull the breaths in and out through your nose.
4. Do four sets of the five breaths, that is, four sets of four short breaths followed by one long breath without stopping, for a total of twenty breaths.

Merge the inhale with the exhale so the breath is connected without any pauses. One inhale connected to one exhale equals one breath. All twenty breaths are connected in this manner so you have one series of twenty connected breaths with no pauses.

Consciously pull the inhale in a relaxed manner and let go completely on the exhale, while continuing to keep the inhale and exhale the same length. Use the short breaths to emphasize the connecting and merging of the inhale and the exhale into unbroken circles. Use the long breath to fill your lungs as completely as you comfortably can on the inhale, and to let go completely on the exhale.

Breathe at a speed that feels natural for you. It is important that the breathing be free, natural, and rhythmical, rather than forced or controlled. This is what enables you to breathe prana as well as air.

Since most of you have developed bad breathing habits, you might experience some physical sensations, such as light-headedness or tingling sensations in your hands or elsewhere. If you do this exercise daily, you will notice that the sensations may change and become less overwhelming, and more generative of healing. This indicates that you are learning about breathing consciously and are getting direct benefits in your body.

Daily practice of this exercise will teach you more about breathing than you have ever learned in your entire life.

If you wish to accelerate the process, contact a professional rebirther and schedule a series of one- to two-hour guided sessions.

Alternate Nostril Breathing

Inhale through the left nostril and exhale through the right nostril. Then inhale through the right nostril and exhale through the left nostril. Repeat this cycle three or nine times. Make the breaths as long as you comfortably can. You can either hold the inhale, or you can connect the inhale to the exhale as in twenty connected breaths.

This exercise came to me from Leonard, who received it from Goraknath. Goraknath said that this exercise, when practiced daily, along with *Om Namaha Shivai*, is enough to keep a constant flow of life energy in the body and create immortality.

This exercise cleans the *nadis*, a series of organs inside the nostrils which send life energy to all the organs of the body.

Do this exercise three or nine times a day for three months in order to experience a cleaning of the internal organs of the nostrils (nadis). Then do it for as long as you want to keep your body.

Water

Water purification means bathing twice a day to clean the energy body as well as the physical body. This can be done either by showers or by total immersion in a tub, the latter being a more efficient method of cleaning the energy body.

The process can be greatly enhanced with the addition of rebirthing. This, however, is a very advanced form of spiritual purification, and you must be ready for it. The minimum qualification, as noted, is ten dry sessions with a well-trained rebirther.

Water purification as an initiation into the spiritual life is an ancient practice—it is called baptism and it was in use long before the Christians began practicing it. Now we have the convenience of indoor plumbing and hot water heaters. Breathing while bathing in warm water produces different results than breathing while immersed in cold water. Leonard likes to point to modern plumbers as the saviors of the world. He says, "If you have hot running water, a bathtub and a fireplace, you have the most sophisticated immortal yogi cave imaginable." He's right, of course.

Fire

In the Biblical book of Genesis, God promises Noah that the Earth will never be destroyed by flood again. He makes a covenant with Noah to seal this promise, saying that the rainbow will be the symbol of this covenant. The Bible says the next time the Earth is destroyed it will be by fire. In the New Testament book of II Peter there is a verse that says: "But the day of the Lord will come as a thief in the night; in which the heavens shall pass away with a great noise, and the elements shall melt with fervent heat, the earth also and the works that are therein shall be burned up."[2]

If you believe the events of 1972, then you know we would have been destroyed by fire had not the Sirians intervened. We were not evolved enough to just tune to the energy of the sun.

Fire is the most neglected of the elements. We are dangerously out of touch with it, and when we are out of touch with an element it can destroy us. Less than a century ago, fire was necessary for cooking and to provide warmth. Now we have central heating and microwaves. This is the same technology that is choking us with the internal combustion engine, and it is the same technology that has given us guns and weapons of mass destruction. All are examples of the mis-use of the fire principle.

Fire purification means developing a conscious relationship to fire so you notice experientially what the fire is doing for you.

The word "chakra" means wheel. Your wheels of energy are always turning. When you are by a fire, they are turning through the flames.

Fire is the most efficient element for burning away anger and the death urge, the basic principle being anything that is not God gets burned away.

Being outdoors with an open fire in a pit is the best. Next comes a fireplace or a wood-burning stove. If you have neither, use candles. Candles are much more subtle, but they are beautiful in the cathedral-type effect they produce. Four candles produce many times the benefit of one candle.

When you are learning the secrets of fire you initially have to spend a lot of time with it, five to ten hours recommended. After you have learned fire's lessons, it takes less time. You need to discover experientially what fire is all about. When you are experiencing your energy body, and you have developed a conscious relationship with fire, you have learned its secrets.

The basic fire ceremony consists simply of offering portions of your food to the fire while saying *Om Namaha Shivai Swaha*. "Swaha" means "I offer" or "I am one with." It is to make yourself one with the energy of the fire and one with God.

In closing, I include two other methods of spiritual purification.

The first, shaving your head, is an advanced form of purification. Your crown chakra is constantly being impressed by programs that are encoded in your hair. When you shave your head, it is no longer receiving those old impressions. Shaving brings dramatic results that can be either positive or negative—but it must be done consciously.

The second is meditating on the full moon. Babaji says the full moon has the power to heal anything. I began practicing this meditation in June of 1981 while attending a four-day rebirthing workshop. I attended the workshop during the day, and watched the moon at night. At one point, a few hours into the second night, the moon turned into Babaji's face. I have had a special relationship with the moon ever since.

Notes

1. John Robbins, *Diet for a New America* (Walpole, NH: Stillpoint Publishing, 1987).

2. The Holy Bible (New York: Oxford University Press), II Peter, Ch. 3, Verse 10.

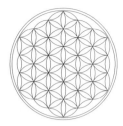

17

BABAJI

Babaji is a Sanskrit word meaning "the ruling father." Babaji usually refers to himself as Bhole Baba, which means "simple father." He almost always lives as a *sadhu*. Again, a *sadhu* is a person who gives up worldly possessions in order to dwell in Nature and practice spiritual purification on a full time-basis.

In June 1970, Babaji manifested a body. He appeared in a cave at the foot of Mount Kailash near the village of Herakhan in a remote spot in the Himalayan Mountains.

According to *Teachings of Babaji, Volume II:*

> He had no known parents or family, he appeared as a youth of 18 or so, yet he displayed great wisdom and power—divine powers—from the start. Some Hairakhan villagers saw him as an old man with a long, white beard; others as a young man with a long beard; others as a beautiful young man with no beard. Two men spoke to him at the same time—one saw an old man with a beard, the other saw a young man with no beard. He was seen in different places at the same time. He knew the scriptures and could quote them in Sanskrit as well as in Hindi, yet there is no evidence of his having been "educated." He ate almost nothing for months on end—two or three years—yet his energy was boundless.[1]

In September of 1970 Babaji climbed to the top of Mount Kailash and sat in the same position for forty-five days without moving—no food, no exercise, no bathroom breaks, and no talking (Fig. 17-1).

Babaji has appeared in many different ways and forms throughout human history. He first appeared as Shiva, then Ram, then Krishna. His most public manifestation, according to Leonard, was as Goraknath. It was Goraknath who gave immortality to Bhartriji in 56 BC, and also to Bhartriji's nephew Gopichand. Leonard says Goraknath has trained more immortals than anyone. When Babaji was Goraknath, he blessed a tree in Kathmandu. The tree rains blossoms continuously from four AM to four PM every day.

Between 1800 and 1922 Babaji was known as Herakhan Baba. He appeared to villagers in 1800 out of a ball of light, and left the same way in 1922. From 1924 to 1958, he lived as a simple yogi.

One rebirther friend of mine had a picture of Babaji. She said she had mixed feelings about Babaji because of her involvement in the Self-Realization Fellowship (founded by Paramahansa Yogananda). When she got involved in rebirthing she was very excited, thinking she could actually meet Babaji, but the Self-Realization Fellowship was very negative about her enthusiasm, insisting that he was not the same Babaji!

After she became a rebirther her picture of Babaji—her favorite picture—spontaneously combusted.

Every time Babaji makes a historical appearance, people get hung up on that body. One time when Leonard was hiking in Herakhan he met a middle-aged man and his father. The father was a devotee of Herakhan Baba in his old form. The son was a devotee of Babaji in his new form. In spite of the fact that the father had met Babaji in his new form, whenever he meditates, Babaji appears to him in his Herakhan

Figure 17-1

Baba form. The father and son worship Babaji in two different forms yet they both know he is the same person.

Leonard tells another story of Babaji appearing in two forms simultaneously, with both forms having a following. The two forms, Goraknath and Alama Pravo, met and had a contest, which went as follows: Goraknath handed Alama Pravo a sword and said, "Take this sword and cut me in two." Alama Pravo took the sword and, with all of his might, came down on Goraknath's head. Nothing happened.

Alama Pravo then gave the sword to Goraknath and said, "Now cut me." Goraknath put the sword right through Alama Pravo's body. Nothing happened. It didn't even cut his clothes.

Goraknath was the side of Babaji that is the manifestation of strength and power, while Alama Pravo was the side of Babaji that is the manifestation of emptiness and clarity. To this day, devotees in both camps feel that their guru won. Some of them got the message.

Leonard tells another Babaji story from *Bhagwan Shri Haidakhan Wale Baba*, by Giridhari Lai Mishra, p. 50:

> Once Haidakhan Baba (in His "old" form) was travelling with a devotee (Jeevanchand Joshi) to Badrinath (a religious pilgrim centre). En route, the devotee was struck by cholera. After a violent but short period of vomiting and profuse dysentery, he was very close to breathing his last.
>
> Babaji, compassionate as ever, felt sorry for him and said, "I shall leave My body instead of you, as there is no one to mourn my loss." The attack of cholera subsided immediately, as far as the devotee was concerned; but Babaji, on the other hand, was hit by the same disease very quickly and told the devotee, "When I leave My body, consign the lifeless form to the flames and the 'ashes' to the Ganges." Shortly afterward, He left the human body. The devotee, grief-stricken though he was, did as he had been instructed by Babaji.
>
> Shortly thereafter, the devotee returned to his hometown of Almora. On arrival at his house, he was informed that Shri Babaji was staying, for the last few days, at

another devotee's house. It was impossible to believe
that this could be true, as he had himself done the last
rites. Nevertheless, he hastened to this devotee's house.
Lo and behold! Babaji was sitting there in person. He
did not even believe his eyes until he felt Babaji's body.

The entire episode so shocked the devotee that he
was practically insane for about six months.[2]

Babaji stopped his heart on Valentine's Day 1984. In so
doing, he mirrored the most popular way of dying on the planet
today. He said his body is for us; he only came to serve. Just as
he only apparently died to Joshi, he also only apparently died
on February 14, 1984. He immediately reassembled a new body.

He had his body buried, and it did not decay. It was as
healthy from a physiological standpoint on the day he was
buried as on the day he died. Some of the people present at
his burial said that after his body was covered by about a
foot of dirt, the dirt suddenly fell in. When they filled the
grave, it was concave. This implies that he dematerialized his
body when it was buried.

Babaji promised he would return in physical form to Herakhan in 1989. I don't know if it happened. In the mean-
time, a picture of him was taken in Belgium on May 1, 1986.
Some of Leonard's friends in India asked Sai Baba where
they could find Babaji. He told them, and they went to the
place and found Babaji in physical form. Leonard later found
him too.

Many of Babaji's followers would tell you that Babaji is
the eternal manifestation of God in human form. Leonard
insists that this is true. I am simply presenting you with the
information; I will let you decide for yourself. I offer two
more quotes from *Teachings of Babaji, Volume II:*

Most of Shri Babaji's followers experience and worship
him as a true, ageless manifestation of God. The big and

little miracles he performed daily in the lives of his followers, his reading and responding to their thoughts
before they were uttered, his healing, his guidance, his
teachings are at a level beyond even advanced human
ability. The dramatic, external miracles were infrequent;
most of his miracles occurred in the mind, hearts and
lives of his followers—miracles of understanding, guidance, teaching and support when, where and as needed.[3]

To those who asked, Hairakhan Baba sometimes
acknowledged that he is the Shiva Mahavatar Babaji,
known to hundreds of thousands in the world through
Paramahansa Yogananda's *Autobiography of a Yogi*. A
mahavatar is a human manifestation of God, not born
of a woman.[4]

My personal experience of Babaji began, as I indicated
earlier, when I first met Leonard in 1979 and purchased a
poster of Babaji.

Notes
    1. *Teachings of Babaji, Vol. II* (Haidakhan, District Nainital, U.P.,
India: Haidakhandi Samaj, Haidakhan Vishwamahadham), Fore-
word, p. iii.
    2. Leonard Orr, *Physical Immortality for Christians* (Sierraville,
CA: I Am Alive Now Project), p. 85.
    3. *Teachings of Babaji*, Vol. II, Foreword, p. v.
    4. Ibid., p. iii.

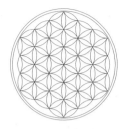

18

THE HIGHER SELF

One day in January of 1996 I came home to find a message on my answering machine. It was from Debra Evans, the program director of the Whole Life Expo. She wanted to know if I would be willing to be on their channeling panel since I was already a featured speaker at the Expo.

I returned the call with my answer firmly in mind. I said, "Thank you for asking, but you should know that I'm not a channel. I don't channel anybody; furthermore, not one word in my book is channeled." I thought that would certainly do it, but she wasn't so easily convinced. We talked for a while, and I began to tell her what I do. "What I'm really about," I said, "is connecting with the higher self." We continued to talk and I explained in greater detail what I meant by that. Then she said, "That's perfect, you'll be great!"

So I was going to be on the channeling panel. All of a sudden I decided that I had better figure out what I was going to say. As I thought about it, my mind wandered back to May 1980, when I was at Campbell Hot Springs, Leonard Orr's rebirthing center in the Sierra, with Leonard and twenty-five to thirty of his students. We were training to become rebirthing and workshop leaders.

187

The plan was to go to Europe with Leonard in June, where we would give two weeks of rebirthing training in a particular country and then move on to the next country. The final destination would be India in September to visit Babaji.

I knew that I was not going to Europe. I didn't have the money, I didn't want to miss a summer at home hiking, and Billy Martin was the new manager of the Oakland A's—and I was all pumped up for that. I just did not want to go and I was certain of it! So I met with Leonard to tell him of my decision. He smiled, looked me straight in the eyes, and said, "Come to Europe."

That was it. There was something about that communication—nothing like it has happened with Leonard before or since. It felt like Babaji was speaking through Leonard. I knew instantly in every cell of my body that I was going to Europe.

I didn't make a Babaji connection at the time, and it took me a while to consider the possibility. What I did notice was all the energy in Leonard's group centered around Babaji and that going to India was the "in" thing to do. Many rebirthers had already made the trek, all of whom returned with shaved heads and incredible stories.

I didn't know if the stories were true, but I was definitely caught up in the wonder of it all, so I withheld judgment. I was just beginning to tune into the creative power of thought, and I recognized the importance of being open to the possibility—smart choice.

One friend I was to meet a few years later was convinced that Babaji was nothing but a fat old man who actually did have a heart attack on February 14, 1984. And the beauty of it is, he is right! Babaji will appear to you any way you want. Babaji said, "If you come to me with doubts, I will give you every reason to doubt." He also said, "If you come to me with love, I will show you more than you have ever known."

Then I recalled the inner voice, the inner communication that began spontaneously while I was in Sweden. I was in the midst of chaos, confusion, and turmoil; I had only enough money to purchase a one-way ticket to London. That meant I had to earn my way as I went, teaching to others as I was just learning myself. My old world had fallen completely apart, none of the securities and comforts were left, and I was clueless as to what the new one would be like.

Yet, included in this chaos was an inner voice that suddenly appeared telling me that everything was okay. That "voice" stayed with me throughout the trip. Chaos and confusion were still present, but somehow I had a shifted relationship to them. I felt an inner calmness, like being in the eye of the hurricane.

Then came mid-August. Four or five of us had separated from the main group and we were in Amsterdam. I don't remember where Leonard was. Because I was away from the group, I no longer had a source of income. I didn't even have enough money to get back home, and I was becoming desperate. I wanted to go home more than anything!

Then I heard about a possibility from a friend. He told me of a courier, DHL, that offered free transportation to New York in exchange for your luggage space. I called them and was told that there was only one free trip a day, but I could be placed on a waiting list. There was no possibility, they said, of an opening for at least two months.

The news was most depressing. Here I was stranded in Amsterdam, with no idea how or if I would ever get home. For some reason, I decided to call DHL back the next day. This time I was told of a situation that, as they said, "never happens." There was a last-minute cancellation for that day and if I could get to the airport right away, I could get the flight. I never moved so fast in my life. I said, "Thank you, Babaji" and was on my way!

When I got to New York I discovered that the airlines were in the midst of a price war, and I was able to get from New York to San Francisco for $99. When I got home to the west coast, I felt I had failed in the sense that I would not be going to India to meet Babaji. But it didn't matter, I was so happy to be home. As it turned out, while the rest of the group went to India to meet Babaji, I went home to meet him.

Back in California, the inner voice not only continued, but began to take on a different form.

One day I noticed my cat Freddie was paralyzed in the lower half of his body. I observed it for a few days. He was in no pain, yet he was half-paralyzed. I was very concerned. At the time I had four cats, two adults and two kittens, all of whom were my favorites, but Freddie was my favorite favorite. So I took him to the vet, who had never seen an affliction like it. He had no idea, no clue.

I took Freddie home, feeling depressed and very emotional about the situation. Then something happened, totally spontaneously. I began to feel with increasing certainty in every passing second that there was no reason, absolutely no reason, that Freddie couldn't be perfectly healthy. I didn't stop to think about this. It wasn't premeditated, it just happened.

In one flashing moment I knew that and felt it with greater certainty than I have ever known anything. In an instant, he was healed.

Freddie came home one day shortly thereafter with one eyelid shut. It remained that way for two or three weeks. When it finally opened it looked like a piece of rotten meat—completely void of life and ugly, very ugly. I took him back to the same vet who again was clueless. He told me that the eyeball would almost certainly have to be removed, and soon.

So I took Freddie home and began preparing for the inevitable. I was really in a funk this time. Then the same thing happened again. I did not sit down and think about doing what I did last time. It just happened. I was sitting with Freddie and I began to think, to sense, to feel the eyeball in a state of perfect health. It got stronger and stronger until I felt it and knew it with total certainty. Then in an instant, the eyeball was healed.

I took him back to the vet, just to be sure. The possibility that the eyeball could be perfectly healthy again was not in this vet's belief system. His mind was completely blown. Freddie never again had a problem with paralysis or with his eye.

Throughout the entire experience, I knew it was Babaji, I just knew it!

So as I was preparing my talk for the channeling panel, it hit me: Of course, that was my initial contact with my higher self! The higher self isn't out to scare you or trick you; to the contrary, it will appear to you in a way that you are best able to accept and align with. For me it was Babaji. Great—it only took me sixteen years to figure that out!

What is the higher self? Let me begin by telling you how Drunvalo's angels first described it to him. They said, suppose you are on a river in a canoe. It's a beautiful day, and you're having a great time paddling down the river. All of a sudden, the higher self comes in and says to take your canoe over to the shore and carry it through the woods. That might seem rather inconvenient, and you might wonder why.

Inconvenience, however, means nothing to the higher self. So if you have learned to follow the higher self, you will take your canoe out of the water even though it makes no sense to you at the time. Then in retrospect you will understand.

Even though the higher self isn't all-knowing, it certainly has a greater perspective than we do. In this story, the higher self is able to fly a few hundred feet above the ground, and is able to see beyond the bends in the river. It was able to observe a 500-foot waterfall beyond the next bend!

The question then is: How do you connect with your higher self? For me, it was something that just seemed to happen. I didn't plan it, I didn't ask for it, I didn't even know there was such a thing.

It happened to me in a way remarkably similar to Drunvalo's experience. Back in May of 1970, at exactly the same time, we both "gave up" on life.

I had turned twenty-six, I was no longer eligible for the draft, and I no longer had any need for my job. I was a mathematics teacher in the public school system for my first three years out of college. I had taken the job for only one reason—Vietnam! I didn't belong; I felt like a fish out of water. When my twenty-sixth birthday came, I said, "That's it. I'm going to quit teaching and do what I've always wanted to do!" For me, that initially meant giving the professional bowlers' tour a try. Then it meant moving to California. Hanging out in Nature soon became my favorite pleasure. So I connected with Nature; I tuned to it, really for the first time. Out of that, I rediscovered my innocence and childlike nature. Everything flowed from that.

Many years later I discovered that Drunvalo had done a similar thing. In May of 1970 he was in the final stages of earning his degree from the University of California at Berkeley. He said he was very tired and didn't know if he could finish. Then came Kent State and the riots that followed. The college system was shut down nationwide and everyone was given B's. So he graduated.

Drunvalo, too, gave up on life as a result of Vietnam and all that was going on at the time. He decided to do what he had always wanted to do. He went to Canada and settled literally in the middle of nowhere in British Columbia. He too connected with Nature and rediscovered his innocence and childlike self.

Then one day two angels appeared to him, one green and one purple. They said they were him. At the time he had no idea what they meant by that. But out of this meeting he began a relationship with his angels that continues to this day.

So for Drunvalo, meeting his higher self was in the form of two angels. For me it was Babaji. And for both of us, it just seemed to happen—and it took me sixteen years to figure it out!

Drunvalo developed an exercise to teach people to connect with higher self. His instructions are: Put a sheet of paper on a clipboard and a pen beside you. Begin the fourteen-breath meditation (the one described in the "Prana" chapter in *Nothing*). Let yourself go deeply into the meditation, then after about twenty minutes, ask to connect with higher self. Ask the higher self to give you a message in a way that lets you know you have made contact. When you get a response, immediately place all ten fingers on the ground. This brings you out of meditation quickly. Then pick up the clipboard and pen and write down uncensored exactly what the message was.

Drunvalo noticed that this exercise only worked for about half the people in his workshops, and he wondered why. He concluded that he must have incomplete information and asked for the rest.

Then in one of his workshops, a Hawaiian of the Huna tradition supplied the missing information. He said the higher self, like everything, exists in threeness—the higher self, the lower self, and the middle self. He said that in order to make a higher-self connection, you must first connect with the lower self; there is no other way.

The lower self, as it turns out, is a child of two to four years old. You connect with it by being childlike, by dropping all of your sophistication and reconnecting with your innocence and with Nature. Then, when the timing feels right, you can ask lower self if you are ready to connect with higher self. It might say yes, it might say no. If it says yes, great! If it says no, just go back to being innocent and childlike.

When you do make connection with higher self, the connection will always be in a form that you can comfortably accept. Drunvalo says he is very visual, so for him it was two large angels. I am not, so for me it was an internal communication—a feeling or a vibration more than anything. However, at one point, Babaji actually did appear to me, and it was in a way I could totally accept.

I was sitting in my room meditating on a poster of him, the one I got in 1979 when I first met Leonard. I began to spontaneously tune to it, merging with the poster until I was one with it. Then a voice inside me asked, "Babaji, was it you?"

I was thinking of all that had happened. I went back to May and my exchange with Leonard. Leonard had said that Babaji gave him special powers that he uses on occasion. I wondered if it was Babaji coming through then. I thought of all that had transpired in Europe and the inner voices.

If these were coincidences, they were pretty good. So I wondered if that was Babaji. Then I thought about Freddie. Throughout all of these events, I intuitively knew it was Babaji, and now I was asking for confirmation.

All of a sudden the likeness of Babaji in the poster became alive and animated, like a cartoon character. He started dancing around; he looked at me, smiled, and nodded in the affirmative. I got the message.

To this day, I have that poster. It continues to come to life for me every time I look at it. It's the cover of this book, by the way. I thought you might like to see it.

Following higher self is really about learning to follow the spirit within rather than external authority. The feedback is instant—it is always in the moment, and always accurate. It may, however, be inconvenient, for inconvenience means nothing to higher self. It was extremely inconvenient for me to go to Europe, but so what? It was the doorway for a whole new possibility. My life has never been the same. Possibilities that otherwise never could have existed have opened up for me as a result.

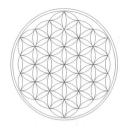

19

THE FLOWER OF LIFE

The Image

To the untrained eye, the flower of life (Fig. 19-1) looks like an interesting pattern. Closer inspection reveals nineteen perfectly interwoven circles, truly a geometric miracle. But would you ever guess that this image is the blueprint for all of creation; that contained within this pattern is literally everything—all laws of physics, all biological life forms—including all of us? Probably not. Dan Winter has conclusively shown that even emotions have geometrical shapes associated with them.

The image of the flower of life contains all of sacred geometry, the geometrical patterns that Nature uses to create *everything* in this reality.

One of the images contained within the flower of life is known as the fruit of life (Fig. 19-2). Thirteen systems of information come out of the fruit of life. Each of these thirteen systems produces a set of geometries that delineate and describe in detail every single aspect of our reality.

You get to these thirteen systems of information by combining female energy with male energy. In sacred geometry, curved lines are female while straight lines are male. One of

Figure 19-1. The flower of life.

these thirteen systems is created by connecting the centers
of all the spheres in the fruit of life. If you do, you come up
with a figure known as Metatron's Cube (Fig. 19-3).

Contained within Metatron's Cube are the five Platonic
solids (Fig. 19-4). The criteria for Platonic solids are that all
their edges are equal; they have only one surface and one
angle; and their points all fit on the surface of a sphere. There
are only five known shapes that can do this.

These five figures are of enormous importance, as they
are the key to many patterns found throughout our reality.
They are also the components of the energy fields around
our bodies. One of these fields around our bodies is in the
form of a star tetrahedron, and it is contained in Metatron's
Cube (Fig. 19-5 and Fig. 19-6).

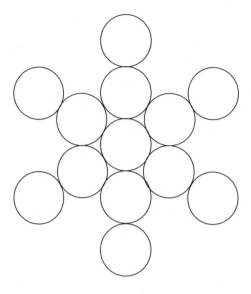

Figure 19-2. The fruit of life.

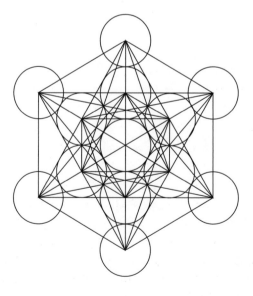

Figure 19-3. Metatron's Cube.

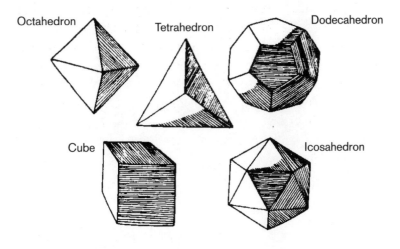

Figure 19-4. The five Platonic Solids.

Figure 19-5. The star tetrahedron extracted
from Metatron's Cube.

There is also a tube that runs through the center of the body, connecting the apexes of the star tetrahedral field.

Before we fell in consciousness 13,000 years ago, we breathed prana through this tube. Prana simultaneously comes in from the top and passes through the pineal gland, and enters from the bottom, meeting in one of the chakras. Remembering how to breathe through this tube, combined with rotating the fields around the body, produces the merkaba, a vehicle of ascension.

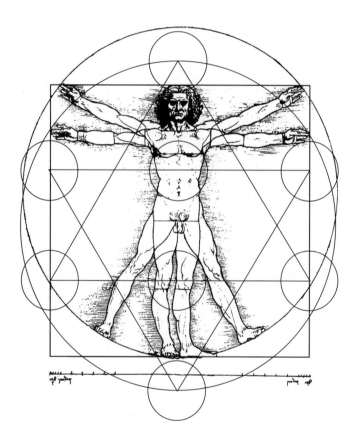

Figure 19-6. The star tetrahedral fields around our bodies.

There are actually three star tetrahedral fields superimposed over each other around the body. One is the physical body, one is the mental body, and the third is the emotional body. This is literally so. The fields are rotated by linking together the mind, the emotions, and the physical body. The mental field spins to the left, the emotional field to the right, and the field for the body remains stationary. When these fields are rotated at very specific speeds and in a certain way, a disk pops out at the base of the spine for fifty-five to sixty feet and a sphere appears. It looks like a flying saucer.

This field is known as the merkaba. It is the original creation pattern of the universe on all levels of existence. It is how we got here and it is how we will leave.

The word "Mer" means counter-rotating fields of light; "Ka" spirit; and "Ba" is body or reality. So the Mer-Ka-Ba is a counter-rotating field of light that takes both body and spirit with it. Once you know how to activate these fields you can use your merkaba to travel throughout the universe.

The bottom line on the Flower of Life workshop is the teaching of the merkaba and the activation of this field so that it can, at the appropriate time, be used as a vehicle of ascension.

The Workshop

In the "Completion" chapter in my first book, I told of my experiences in attending the Flower of Life workshop in April 1994 in Austin, Texas, led by Drunvalo, and what an incredible experience of unity consciousness it was. This was the last time Drunvalo gave the workshop.

I also told of Drunvalo's decision to turn the workshop over to trained facilitators, and of my interest in becoming one. I realized that I was well qualified to give this workshop. My many years as a rebirther and workshop leader had prepared me in leading people through the many changes I knew they would go through in the course of such a workshop.

From my own experience and from what I observed in the Austin workshop, I know that it puts you through many changes. The key is to provide a setting of awareness, safety, and trust in order to facilitate for people the process of moving through and integrating these changes. That is fundamentally important. Without that, there is no workshop.

So I returned to Austin in June of the same year and took a nine-day facilitator training. But I waited almost one year before I gave my first workshop.

I had decided some time earlier that instead of sitting back and wondering what I could do that I would make it my personal business to ensure that our transition from one world to the next is a gentle one. That meant taking an all-inclusive approach; it meant finding a way to be effective in a you-and-me world to, as Werner Erhard said, "discover what is needed and wanted and then to produce it."[1] That meant finding a way to empower others. I wanted to be sure that giving the Flower of Life workshop was the right vehicle.

I was also in the final stages of letting go, of moving from conditioned motivation into divine motivation. I wanted to wait for my first book to come out, and I also wanted to see if what I was doing was real. If it wasn't, no amount of forcing the issue would work. If it was, all I had to do was sit back and allow it to happen.

I remembered Drunvalo discussing how when he first gave the Flower of Life workshop, Thoth told him to pick a remote location. That way, people with one hundred percent intention would be there, while those who weren't ready wouldn't even know there was a workshop. I liked that idea, and knowing that what the participants bring to the workshop is everything, I decided to make my workshop known primarily by word of mouth, and to those who had read my book and written to me.

It was Arnold Patent who said, "The Universe handles the details."[2] He also said, "When you are on purpose, the phone rings and you don't have to dial." The phone did begin to ring. People called and wrote to me from everywhere, and from that, I began to give the workshop.

It took me three workshops to get the kinks out, and to learn how to manage my own energy. I was totally wiped out after each of the first three workshops.

I didn't think it was possible to re-create the experience of unity I had seen in the Austin workshop, and I didn't even try. But some powerful seeds were planted, and by the fourth workshop, it just began to happen. Then it began to *really* happen, and it has since gone off the scale!

The workshop is a six-day experience. About half the time is spent with Drunvalo transmitting the bulk of the information via video. I initially had some doubts about half a workshop being on video, until I realized that all the pieces were in place, and that it was actually possible to do it better this way.

I have worked with many partners in the past and have had many good experiences working this way. But Drunvalo, as it turns out, is the best partner I have ever had. Even though he is on tape, his style comes through in a way that enables everyone to have a delightful and complete experience of him. Furthermore, I know exactly what he is going to say and when he is going to say it (he is on tape, after all), so I can work with him to maximum benefit.

This creates an excellent foundation, because the workshop really happens when the video is turned off. It is the sharing, the group discussion, the individual and collective processing of energy, the teaching of the merkaba, and the merkaba meditation where the workshop really happens.

Because the workshop is by nature experiential, it is difficult to recreate that experience in book format.

In thinking about this chapter I realized that the best way to describe the workshop is to let it come alive through the descriptions of past participants. So one day in September of 1996 I invited a group of Flower of Life graduates to come together and share their experiences for a video I was making. Carol Kemp, Brian Hall, Eileen Bray, and Carolyn (last name withheld) had taken the workshop in May of that year, while Paul White took it in April. What follows is a synopsis of their discussion:

> *Carol:* Literally the book fell into my hands. . . . I ate it up, it felt very true to me and I needed more . . . I contacted Bob . . . within a week I was in San Francisco taking the workshop and it was a very powerful experience for me; learning the merkaba, listening to Drunvalo, the interaction with all the people. . . . Since the workshop—activating the merkaba fields—my life is much more joyous than ever. I have a much higher sense of connection with everything and I'm learning more and more how powerful my thoughts are, and how on top of it I must be with my thinking patterns.
>
> . . . As we raise our consciousness the Earth is also raising its consciousness; as we heal ourselves we are helping the Earth heal because we are one. . . . As we raise ourselves up out of the muck, things become lighter. . . . I see it happening in my own life as I heal myself. I see around me things healing, people healing. It's very obvious to me, especially my eight-year-old son. As I change myself he goes through these incredible changes himself and is able to drop all this stuff that I've put on him . . . I'm very aware of that in the last few months.

. . . The heart work is the most important thing. I'm talking about unconditional love, learning how to love and forgive yourself and be able to forgive all these other things that are going on and send out love. . . . I'm talking about compassion and truly understanding where people are coming from.

. . . You can read the book and get the great information. Then if you go to the workshop there is a whole other level to it experientially. Then you go home and continue on your journey . . . experiencing more and more, and hopefully it never stops.

Paul: The book fell off the shelf for me at the bookstore. It was an interesting experience reading it; it kind of read itself. Within about one day I was back at the bookstore purchasing a number of copies for the people I work with. I'd have to say that my one goal after reading the book was to see if I could find Bob and get in touch with him, which wasn't too hard, and set up a time to come to the class. It was really quite a wonderful experience. My life has been, in the last number of years, going through a transformational process, and this was coming to a cusp that sent me exponentially into another realm. So it's been quite a lot of joy from that point forward. It has affected my life in my working relationships with people. I've drawn other people in that are of like mind and seeking experiences to grow in spiritual ways, and finding much more depth of experience than I would have imagined possible. It has touched me in a major way.

. . . I have been learning quite a bit about the power of belief, of good and evil, which brings up judgment and shame, and lots of powerful concepts that we can get sucked into in our lives, and of course the big one, fear, which can take you down any path that you don't want to go. The one thing that seems to balance it out is love. It's a very powerful thing to be able to know that you are free and to be able to express love—and to be able to look at everything else as contrasts, light and dark, rather than good and evil. . . . The basic thing is that you can always bring yourself back to balance, and probably the largest balance that I've been able to know in my own life has been to learn more about how to love. It is evidenced in the workshop; it's the basis for more truth; and I think it's important for everyone to look at in their own lives.

Carolyn: I took the class and I was absolutely blown away. It was six days of putting everything together into a package, but the way it was put together, the way the class was run, the way the videos worked, and the lessons and stories told and the facts that were unfolded in the workshop were what was so mind-blowing because it put it together so easily, so perfectly, so factually. There's no way you can deny that what he is teaching is true, there's just no way and that's why I'd like to share it with people.

One of the most important things that I took away from the class was Drunvalo's suggestion that the one thing you can do for yourself, the planet, and the entire universe is to heal your fear and work on your character. As I've been doing that . . . as I'm healing myself, I see everyone around me changing . . . as you get clearer and drop away more baggage, you heal yourself and the Earth and everybody moves forward and up.

. . . The most phenomenal thing anyone can do is come to the class, because it brings everything together and makes it a full picture, with details that expound more than you can imagine. Reading Bob's book is an excellent general overview, and then taking the course for six days in a row, working with the people you come together with, is incredible. And then you get to start working on yourself. It always comes back to yourself . . . taking responsibility instead of blaming others. Bring it back to yourself and see how you manipulated that to happen so that you could learn something from it. Once you learn from it then you can let it go. For me, that's the most important thing. That class really zeroed in on that and sent me off like a rubber band.

Brian: A friend turned me on to *Nothing*. It's sort of required reading for any UFO enthusiast. It's one of those books that just doesn't tell you about ETs or flying saucers, it has the potential to change your life. When I got to the last chapter and saw that there was a workshop, I knew I had to do it—it literally called me. I contacted Bob at the last minute for his latest workshop. I just barely made it in and I thought that was real interesting. The group was great, the tapes were great, Drunvalo was excellent. It felt like I was meant to be there. . . .

How I've changed? What I've noticed in myself is that I've realized I am being guided by Spirit every step of the way. That's important for me to realize. I've had a series of interesting adventures and synchronicities that I probably would never have noticed before— they've been wonderful. It's nice to know that there are no accidents . . . and it's a pretty wonderful universe out there.

Eileen: . . . There have been a lot of changes since I've done the workshop. And a lot of synchronicities that have just been blowing my mind right and left. The number-one change is how I perceive the world . . . a much bigger picture, there's something big going on . . . I'm more accepting of the darkness now, not accepting that I want it there, but accepting that it's there and it has a purpose, a timing purpose.

. . . We're in a time right now where we're in an accelerated learning program; it's a universal cosmic accelerated learning program. There are a lot of different catalysts that are being made available to each of us. . . . Bob's book is one of these catalysts, the Flower of Life workshop is another catalyst . . . any of these things that come into your life come in for a purpose, and it can only change your life for the better . . . make you more whole and more of who you really are . . . this multi-dimensional being of love. Love is the ultimate; if you want to move through a lot of stuff, start emanating love from yourself. Listen to your inner guidance, be free, drop the fear, and stand up in love, and you'll see your whole reality change, your whole world. How people react to you will change.

Next, here are two letters I received from workshop participants:

June 11, 1997

Dear Bob,

Ron & I felt very privileged to be able to take the Flower of Life workshop under your instruction in April. This was a major adventure for us & has been a turning point in our lives. We feel we were led by some unseen force to purchase your book & then on to take the workshop. The merkaba meditation is the most comforting yet exciting meditation we have ever done—it truly feels as if you are on a journey home. It creates a sense of calmness, peace & love. We met a wonderful group of people, other seekers of spiritual growth which we otherwise would not have met. Maybe the next time we visit San Francisco we can do some sightseeing. Thanks again for providing this experience for us. Take care & good luck with the new book.

Ron & Carla Benson

Dear Bob,

It [the workshop] has meant everything, because it has shown me everything is why I am here. I am a part of this everything. I thank you once again for bringing it to me, and in helping put this puzzle together again. I believe this information is so important in these times, yet on the other hand, I do know everything is playing itself out as it is supposed to. I hope I am playing out my role as has been ordained, as well. This is just the beginning. Good Luck with the book.

All my best,

Kim Edward Black

In the spring of 1996, I received a letter from Louise Vincent from Québec. Then she called me and told me that she and her sister Marthe would like to come to California to meet me and do some rebirthing.

They came and each had four rebirthing sessions. Then they told me they would like to have *Nothing* translated into French, and they would like me to come to Québec to give a Flower of Life workshop.

So I went to Québec and gave what was, in many ways, the best of all the Flower of Life workshops I have facilitated. There were fifty participants, each with the highest possible intention. As a result, we created a six-day celebration of joy and unity. Then they wanted to know if I would come back and give a rebirthing workshop. I agreed.

The last time I gave a rebirthing workshop was in 1991. I had decided then that rebirthing was just too powerful for most people, that it takes a very high degree of intention and responsibility for it to work. So I decided at that time to teach it only through a series of private sessions. Even though I knew I could now give an updated version of this workshop—emotional-body clearing in the context of the big picture (essentially a four-day experience of this book, with each participant receiving two rebirthing sessions), I still had some apprehensions about returning to Québec and giving a workshop that six years ago I had decided to no longer teach.

What I had not counted on was the incredible power that is generated when a group of like-minded people come together with one hundred percent intention. The workshop was a complete success; the energy level was even higher than any of the Flower of Life workshops. As a result, I have been inspired to continue to give it as long as people want it. Here is a letter from Joyce Pinkerton, one of the participants:

August 3, 1997

Hello Bob,

I hope you are doing well. As for me I am going through a very hard phase that I can't *debloque* for right now. I'm having a hard time contacting what is wrong with this, I can't seem to get my thoughts right so if this letter is going in every direction and mixed up and sad this is me at the moment. But it was important for me to try to get the information you asked to you and time was passing.

Rebirth was a giant step for me into consciousness and continues to be the best tool to help me advance in my discovery of myself.

It would be too long to write all it brought to me in the way of consciousness, there are so many so I'll go with the ones that are the most important.

I guess the most important was contacting this feeling of unity. When I did my second rebirthing with the group, I felt we were one lung breathing together. Another was having the grace to experience for maybe fifteen minutes that everything I am looking for is inside me. It's hard to explain the feeling I experienced except that these moments were the most peaceful in my life. Everything I needed was there; love, security, peace, the feeling of being enveloped and not needing anything, because I am a person who spent her life looking outside myself for nourishment.

I think the most important sentence you keep repeating is to make it OK to feel what we feel. This phrase for me is very important because I've passed my life running from myself, but I know that this is the only way to advance—working with your own feelings when they come up.

Also I've finally found a tool which keeps me in my own power and has made me autonomous and this is what I want in life. It's amazing the energies I *debloque* with rebirth.

I feel great gratitude and love towards you Bob, for the beautiful work you are doing to help open the consciousness in this world. Just seeing the way you work in your workshop and the way you are was a great lesson in itself. God bless you and thank you.

With this I say good-bye for now and I am holding a special place for you in my heart.

With great love and gratitude,

Joyce

Of course, there is a big difference between hearing about a workshop and experiencing a workshop. But these descriptions show that, for these people at least, the experience was one that changed their lives forever.

Notes

1. Werner Erhard, "A World that Works for Everyone" (San Francisco: Erhard Seminars Training, 1980), cassette.

2. Arnold M. Patent, *You Can Have It All* (Piermont, NY: Celebration Publishing, 1984), p. 69.

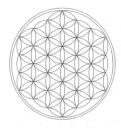

20

UNITY

As indicated in the previous chapter, prior to the fall 13,000 years ago, we were accustomed to breathing in a way that enabled prana to pass through the pineal gland.

This is very significant. It is the way most life breathes. The pineal gland is our connection to the higher dimensional realms and to all life everywhere. It is an eye, our third eye. It is round, hollow, it has a lens for focusing light, and it has color receptors. It has a ninety-degree field of vision, from straight up to straight out, and the light it receives goes to every cell in the body instantaneously.

When we breathed in that manner our experience of the one reality was completely different. We were like cells in a larger body. What was available to one was available to all. That was literally true. Whatever one individual experienced, anyone else was able to re-live by stepping into a holographic recreation of the entire event. It is the dreamtime of the Aborigines in Australia, a remaining example of this type of Unity consciousness on the planet.

Then, as a direct result of a massive misuse of power in Atlantis when the poles and consciousness last shifted, we fell many dimensional levels, from a very high level of awareness down to where we are now, a very low level of awareness.

We stopped breathing in the ancient manner and started taking in the prana through our mouth and nose directly with the air. The prana bypassed the pineal gland, resulting in its non-use for 13,000 years. The direct result of this is separation and polarity consciousness. We experience ourselves as cut off from the rest of life—inside a body looking out at a world that is not us. And we see good and bad, right and wrong.

Simply stated, we are a disharmonic level of consciousness. Given enough time, we will certainly destroy our environment and ourselves. We don't have the awareness to do it any other way. Even though we are dysfunctional, we are absolutely necessary as a stepping stone to get from where we were in Atlantis to where we are going.

The problem in Atlantis was major. It began 16,000 years ago when a group of transplanted Martians tried to take over the planet by creating an external merkaba field. If successful they would have taken control of the planet, but they succeeded only in creating the biggest disaster the planet has ever experienced. The counter-rotating fields of their external merkaba went spinning totally out of control and ripped open other dimensional levels. This caused spirits who were never meant to be here to get pulled in by the millions.

The ascended masters helped a great deal. They were able to repair much of the damage but not all. In essence, they saved the planet, but did not completely heal it.

There were still millions of disembodied beings here who didn't belong. They had to be somewhere, so they inhabited the bodies of the Atlanteans. For the next few thousand years, the situation kept worsening until the place just went crazy.

The ascended masters, looking for an all-inclusive solution, asked for and prayed for help. The answer had to involve everyone, because in the higher aspects of life there is no separation. Everyone and everything is part of the whole. It is only an aspect of our consciousness that causes us to see life as divided.

It was decided by the ascended masters to embark upon a solution that had worked before in similar situations on other planets. The solution was to synthetically initiate a process on the planet that in 13,000 years would give birth to a new level of consciousness—a higher form of Unity consciousness known as Christ-consciousness.

It should be noted that there are five levels of consciousness associated with planet Earth. Each of these levels is related to the number of chromosomes we have in our genetic makeup. Each level has a completely different interpretation of the one reality, and each has a corresponding height range.

The first level, where we were in Atlantis, has forty-two plus two chromosomes and a height range of from three-and-a-half to five feet.

The second level is where we are now. We have forty-four plus two chromosomes and a height range of five to seven feet.

The third level, which is Christ-consciousness, has forty-six plus two chromosomes and a height range of ten to sixteen feet.

The fourth level has forty-eight plus two chromosomes and a height range of twenty-five to thirty-five feet, while the fifth level has fifty plus two chromosomes and a height range of fifty to sixty feet.

The first, third, and fifth levels are differing stages of Unity consciousness while the second and fourth, although disharmonic, are absolutely necessary as stepping stones. Life has never figured out how to go from the first level to the third, or from the third level to the fifth, without first going through the second or fourth levels.

Since the solution to all problems is consciousness, the ascended masters' idea was to get us from the first level of consciousness to the third, and into a higher form of Unity consciousness. Of course, in order to do that, we have had to spend the last 13,000 years on the stepping stone known as the second level.

The third level, or Christ-consciousness, is more advanced than the first level in the sense that you no longer have dream-time; rather, you have realtime—where past, present, and future are all happening at once, and your thoughts and feelings manifest instantly and become the self-generated reality. At this level of awareness, the problems that began in Atlantis would be solved.

There is a new grid around the Earth that is enabling this consciousness to come forth. More than 83,000 sacred sites around the planet, built in very specific places, were used by the ascended masters to create this grid. The process began 13,000 years ago and was completed on February 4, 1989. The grid is electromagnetic in nature, it is located about sixty miles above the Earth, and its geometry is based on the pentagon, as well as a relationship between the dodecahedron and the icosahedron.

We are deeply and literally into the process of moving from one world to another—that is, from the third-dimensional aspect of the Earth to the higher overtones of the fourth dimension of the same planet. That is why we are in the midst of vast changes. At some point in the near future, critical mass will be reached, and the actual dimensional shift will happen.

In fact, the ascended masters were convinced that critical mass was going to happen in the last week of August or the first week of September of 1990. They believed at that time that the necessary number for critical mass—ten percent or five hundred million of the Earth's population—would be reached, that the energy of this critical mass would focus between January tenth to the nineteenth, 1991, and that by the spring of 1991, we would be in a different dimensional level.

Furthermore, because of the speed at which this was occurring, they believed that every last person on the planet would go through ascension at that time. This in itself is incredible. Usually when a planet at our level of development goes through this change, only a very few initially make it to the higher levels of consciousness. The rest of the planet is even bumped down a level or two. Then over a very long period of time, the initial few are able to raise the consciousness of the rest of the planet.

The ascended masters' initial plan was to bond together and leave the planet in one big ball of light. This was intended to be the catalyst that would propel the planet into the higher levels. Obviously this is not what happened. What did happen is that the planet went into a different form of unity, sort of. January 15, 1991, was the date the Gulf War began, where essentially the entire planet unified against one man and one country—not the sort of unity the ascended masters were looking for.

What really happened, according to Drunvalo, is that we *unconsciously* hit critical mass. In a *Leading Edge* interview with Drunvalo on December 22, 1995, he said:

> We as a planet only have a very few people who are actually conscious of what is going on. The number is growing by the minute. Most of the planet was connected to the Christ-grid unconsciously. In their hearts, these people no longer want to live the way that we are living. They don't like the war, rape, murder, and all the garbage that we have now come into. In their hearts, they want to live a simpler, more connected, spiritual way of life, without all this fear. Because so many people have unconsciously connected to this, we reached critical mass a long time ago, but nothing happened—it just kept right on going. It almost happened, but that's

a long story. . . . Where we are now is that we have reached a situation no one has ever seen before, where in the hearts of man almost every person in the world is now connected to the Christ-grid consciousness. There are very few that have not.[1]

The trick now is to reach critical mass consciously. One of the trump cards in this process appears to be the children of the world. Drunvalo says that since 1972, many of the children being born are not ordinary. They are coming from higher levels as part of a greater plan.

In a 1996 interview, Drunvalo said:

When the time does come, as we approach the final days of this era, these children are going to interact in a way that will seem impossible from our point of view. They are going to connect and become one living being. Children all over the world will begin to emanate a vibration that will change the world. It will accelerate everything we're trying to do.[2]

It appears too that the planet is now capable of directly participating—that for the first time in 13,000 years, Mother Earth is awake and her merkaba fields are activated. As Drunvalo said in another recent interview:

She is going to do whatever it takes, and adapt in any way, and give us whatever we need to make sure we are safe and proceed as a planet, as a race, onto the next level. There may be things coming in the future that we could not imagine. Even a little bit further in the future things that would now be considered absolutely impossible will happen.[3]

One possible example of the planet's direct participation is the appearance of plasma-type UFOs in Mexico. I first heard of this in November 1995 at the Fifth Annual International UFO Congress in Mesquite, Nevada. One of the featured speakers, Carlos Dias, had taken several spectacular photos and videos of these brilliant orange-white plasma ships. When scientists in Mexico City analyzed Dias' photographs they found that these ships were attracting energy, not releasing it, and the spectrum of light the ships were giving off was unlike anything they had ever seen.

Dias, who lives in a town one hour south of Mexico City, reported that more than seventy percent of the twenty thousand inhabitants had seen these "lights" in the sky.

Drunvalo, who is also familiar with these UFOs, has said that computer analysis showed these ships to be identical to a human cell. They are living merkaba fields. He said:

> The ship appears to be a living being. They found that as these beings get on a ship, the ship gets bigger. If some get off, the ship gets smaller. Videos of these beings show them walking right through each other. They are just pure light. . . . They are coming out of the world's second largest volcano, south of Mexico City. There are people sitting on the rim of the volcano watching these ships coming out. It is the belief of most of the people down there that they are coming out of inner earth. The dimensional levels go into the Earth just as they go out from the Earth. . . . They have photographs of these beings. They have heads about twenty inches long shaped like an eggplant, with two little antennae, and two small eyes. Their faces are so bright with light that you can hardly see them. They have a tiny little body that is not much bigger than their head. They have

allowed people within thirty feet of them. . . . That's the kind of thing that could jar us into a higher level of consciousness. It could be something right out of science fiction that Mother Earth uses to do this.[4]

The new grid is in place, the planet is awake, and a special light and innocence that have been missing for five hundred years have returned to Nature.

In the spring of 1995 Drunvalo was asked to speak at a Mayan ceremony that had not been performed for more than five hundred years. In his words:

According to the Mayan philosophy, the light of the sun disappeared five hundred and twenty-two years ago and the Earth was plunged into darkness. In the spring of 1995 a new light from the sun, which is a totally different kind of light, began to strike the surface of the Earth for the first time in over five hundred years. . . . From a Melchizedek point of view, this was the sun going from a hydrogen to a helium sun . . . that was producing, literally, a different type of light.[5]

A short time later while in Japan, Drunvalo became acquainted with Shinto, a Japanese Nature-based religion. He discovered that the Mayan and Shinto philosophies have a similar belief regarding the time period of five hundred years ago. The Shinto religion says that Amaterasu, the goddess of the light of the sun, went into the Earth approximately five hundred years ago, and the planet was plunged into darkness.

The Shinto priesthood have a prophecy that a white male from the Four Corners area of the United States would come to their temple near the end of the century, and release this energy.

Drunvalo tells a beautiful story, filled with improbable "coincidences," of how he was the one who initiated the process of Amaterasu, a goddess of great love and innocence, coming forward.

Because of this, we are now able to connect with Mother Earth in a way that previously was not possible. We are now able to become who we truly are, and to demonstrate it, and to make it real.

In closing, I would like to give you in meditation form one of the final keys. I learned this meditation from Drunvalo, but it isn't his—it belongs to all life everywhere. It came from Paramahansa Yogananda's guru, Sri Yukteswar, and according to Drunvalo is one of the final phases of initiation into Kriya yoga.

In order to do this meditation, you need to be aware of your prana tube that begins one hand length above your head and terminates one hand length below your feet. Breathe prana through your tube from above and below, and let it meet in your heart chakra (at your sternum). From there it will radiate into a sphere around your body.

You also need to be aware of the new grid around the Earth. Just know that it is there, and at one point in the meditation, you will connect with it.

Close your eyes. You don't need to know the merkaba, but if you do, go into it, or if you know the Christ-consciousness spherical breathing, go into it; otherwise it doesn't matter.

Relax and take a deep breath, see a white mist as you exhale, and relax into it. Take one more breath and feel your body relaxing.

Place your attention on the tube that runs through your body. With your intention, allow the two ends of the tube to open, and feel the white light of prana come rushing in and meet in your heart and then radiate out into a sphere around you. The flow is continuous, whether you are inhaling or exhaling. Just feel this for a minute.

Now bring your attention to Mother Earth and to Nature and feel the love that you have for her, for the trees, the clouds, the wind, the birds, the animals, the water, the people. Feel the love you have for the Earth and center it in your heart, right where the prana flows are meeting. Bring it into a little sphere.

When you get your love there where you can feel it, send it down to the center of the Earth, and wait for Mother Earth to send back her love for you, up the tube. Wait until you can feel this.

Now place your attention on Father Sky, to all life everywhere; all the stars, the galaxies, all the life in the heavens. Feel your love for the Father, think of looking into a night sky.

Take all your love for Father Sky and put it into your heart, where your love for the Mother is. Keep them separate for a moment. Now send it up and let it connect with the Christ-consciousness grid, about sixty miles above the Earth. Then wait until you feel the love of Father Sky come back.

With the love of Mother Earth and Father Sky in you at the same time, the holy trinity is present—mother, father, and child. When this happens, something very special can take place.

Become aware of the tube again. This time, place your attention on the two ends. Open them even further, and allow all life everywhere, the consciousness of all creation, to enter from both poles, to come into your heart, and to radiate as light around you. Open them up, and allow God to come in, and to form a sphere around your body.

Now allow that sphere to expand, slowly at first. Then let it get bigger and bigger, moving out faster and faster. Finally let it expand uncontrollably, through all dimensions. Let it return back to all life everywhere.

Now you are breathing all life and all life is breathing you.

May your life never again be the same!

Notes

1. *The Leading Edge International Research Journal* (Yelm, WA: Leading Edge Research Group), Issue #88, "Leading Edge Research Group Interviews Drunvalo Melchizedek," Dec. 1995.

2. *Mount Shasta's Directions* (Mount Shasta, CA: Southern Siskiyou Newspapers), Issue 2, Volume 3, "Drunvalo Melchizedek . . . Interview with a Giant," Spring 1996.

3. *The Leading Edge International Research Journal*, Issue #88, Dec. 1995.

4. Ibid.

5. Drunvalo Melchizedek, "An Update on Flower of Life Research" (Pleasanton, CA: Oughten House), cassette of talk given on June 22, 1997, in Pleasanton, CA.

For information regarding Flower of Life and Rebirthing
workshops, write to:

Bob Frissell
c/o North Atlantic Books
P.O. Box 12327
Berkeley, CA 94712

Please include a self-addressed stamped envelope.

INDEX